INTRODUCING ETHICS

FOR HERE AND NOW

James P. Sterba

University of Notre Dame

Boston Columbus Indianapolis New York San Francisco Upper Saddle River
Amsterdam Cape Town Dubai London Madrid Milan Munich Paris Montreal Toronto
Delhi Mexico City São Paulo Sydney Hong Kong Seoul Singapore Taipei Tokyo

Editorial Director: Craig Campanella
Editor in Chief: Dickson Musslewhite
Executive Editor: Ashley Dodge
Editorial Project Manager: Carly Czech
Assistant Editor: Courtney Elezovic
Editorial Assistant: Nicole Suddeth
VP/Director of Marketing: Brandy Dawson
Senior Marketing Manager: Laura Lee
  Manley

Marketing Assistant: Paige Patunas
Production Project Manager: Debbie Ryan
Art Director: Jayne Conte
Cover Designer: Bruce Kenselarr
Digital Media Editor: Rachel Comerford
Editorial Production Service:
  PreMediaGlobal
**Editorial Production and Composition
  Service:** Saraswathi Muralidhar/PreMediaGlobal

Library of Congress Cataloging-in-Publication Data
Sterba, James P.
  Introducing ethics: for here and now/James P. Sterba.—Student edition.
      pages cm
  Includes bibliographical references and index.
  ISBN-13: 978-0-205-22668-9
  ISBN-10: 0-205-22668-X
 1. Ethics—Textbooks.   I. Title.
  BJ1025.S82 2012
  170—dc23
                                                    2011050589

10 9 8 7 6 5 4 3 2 1 CRW 13 12 11 10 09

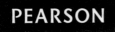

ISBN-10: 0-205-22668-X
ISBN-13: 978-0-205-22668-9

To all my students who helped to make this book possible.

CONTENTS

Preface   ix

Introduction   1
  Why Do We Need This Knowledge?   2
  Three Challenges to Ethics   3
  Three Traditional Ethical Perspectives   4
  Three More Challenges to Ethics   5
  Conclusion   5
    Notes   5

Chapter 1   Religion and Morality   6
  The Euthyphro Question   6
  Medieval Developments of Divine Command Theory   7
  Morality Dependent on God Through Creation   7
  Problems for Divine Command Theory   8
    How Are We to Understand God's Commands?   8
    Are God's Commands Justified by Creation?   9
    How Are We to Identify God's Commands?   10
  Radically Modified Divine Command Theory   11
  Religion and the Public Arena   11
  Is Rawls's Requirement of Public Reason Unfair?   13
    Seeing Different Kinds of Unfairness   14
  Can Religious Moral Teachings Be Required by Reason?   17
  How Public Reasons Are to Be Made Accessible   18
  Conclusion   19
  MySearchLab Connections   19
    Notes   20

Chapter 2   The Challenge of Moral Relativism   22
  Negative Consequences from Endorsing Moral Relativism   23
  Tolerance—A Benefit from Endorsing Moral Relativism?   23
  But Is It True?   25
    Analysis of the Case of Rape and Marriage   28
    Analysis of the Case of Widows and Suttee   30
    Analysis of the Case of Female Circumcision   31

A Comparison to Divine Command Theory 33

The Standard Criticism of Moral Relativism 33

Our Six Purported Cases of Moral Relativism 34

Conclusion 35

MySearchLab Connections 35

Notes 35

Chapter 3 **The Challenge of Egoism** **37**

Psychological Egoism 37

Ethical Egoism 39

Individual Ethical Egoism 39

Universal Ethical Egoism 40

Appealing to Publicity 41

Paralleling Egoism and Racism 41

Appealing to Consistency 42

Is There No Way to Meet the Challenge of Universal
Ethical Egoism? 43

From Rationality to Morality 44

Lifeboat Cases 47

Morality as Compromise 47

Conclusion 48

MySearchLab Connections 48

Notes 48

Chapter 4 **Utilitarian Ethics** **51**

Introducing Utilitarian Ethics 52

An Implication of Utilitarian Ethics: Sacrificing the Few
for the Many 53

Osama Bin Laden and Terrorism 54

Hypothetical Examples 56

An Objection to Utilitarian Ethics: Never Do Evil 57

Refining and Answering the Objection: Necessary Harm
and Independent Reasons 57

A Further Defense: Act Utilitarianism and Rule
Utilitarianism 59

A Better Defense: The "Ought" Implies "Can" Principle 60

Conclusion 62

MySearchLab Connections 63

Notes 63

Chapter 5   **Kantian Ethics   65**

Kant's Categorical Imperative Test   65

Kant, Egoism and Hypothetical Imperatives   66

A Central Requirement of Morality   67

Universalizability Not Enough   68

Other Formulations of Kant's Test   68

Two Interpretations of Kant's Ethics   69

    Welfare Liberalism   69

    Libertarianism   70

Supporting Examples   71

Conflicting Liberties   73

    An Expanded "Ought" Implies "Can" Principle Again   73

    Libertarian Objections   74

Conclusion   76

MySearchLab Connections   76

    Notes   77

Chapter 6   **Aristotelian Ethics   78**

Happiness and the Virtuous Life   78

Characterizing the Virtuous Life   80

Conflicts with Kantian Ethics   81

The Importance of Rules   82

Focusing on How We Should Act   82

The Priority Question   83

Ayn Rand's Aristotelian Ethics   84

The No-Conflict Thesis   85

Conflicts of Self-Interest in Rand's Novels   87

The No-Duty Thesis   88

The Importance of Rejecting the No-Conflict Thesis   89

Conclusion   90

MySearchLab Connections   90

    Notes   91

Taking-Stock Interlude   93

Chapter 7   **The Challenge of Environmentalism   95**

Singer's Utilitarian Environmentalism   95

Regan's Kantian Environmentalism   96

Biocentrism   96

Principles of Conflict Resolution   98

Individualism and Holism   101

An Objection from a Somewhat Alien Perspective   104

Conclusion   106

MySearchLab Connections   107

Notes   107

Chapter 8   **The Challenge of Feminism   109**

Gilligan's Challenge   109

The Practical Inadequacy of Traditional Theories of Justice   111

Is It Discrimination or Is It Choice?   112

The Practical Inadequacy of the Traditional Ideals
of a Morally Good Person   115

Conclusion   118

MySearchLab Connections   119

Notes   119

Chapter 9   **The Challenge of Multiculturalism   122**

Correcting and Interpreting Traditional Ethics   124

Using American Indian Culture   124

Using Confucius   126

New Obligations for Traditional Ethics   128

Applying Traditional Ethics Cross-Culturally   133

Conclusion   135

MySearchLab Connections   136

Notes   136

Conclusion   138

Three Challenges   138

Three Conceptions of Ethics   138

Three More Challenges   139

Practicing Ethics   140

Summing-Up   144

Notes   144

Glossary   145

Index   147

PREFACE

Every day you almost certainly make ethical or moral choices. But do you make them well? This book can help you answer that question. This book begins by considering three challenges to the very possibility that ethics can provide us with useful independent knowledge for making choices: (1) Morality is determined by religion not reason, (2) It's all relative, and (3) It's better to be an egoist. Many people believe that one or more of these challenges are valid and so for that reason alone, they must be considered. If this book is successful in meeting these challenges (you will have to decide whether that is the case), it then makes sense to go on, as the book does, to examine the three main traditional accounts of ethics as independent sources of knowledge that continue to have their contemporary defenders: (1) utilitarian ethics (it is about maximizing utility), (2) Kantian ethics (it is about doing your duty), and (3) Aristotelian ethics (it is about being virtuous) to determine whether one of them is better than the others. (Again, you will have to decide whether a better case can be made for one or another of these perspectives.) This book then takes up three challenges that have been raised to all the traditional conceptions of ethics: (1) the environmental challenge (traditional ethics is biased against nonhuman living beings), (2) the feminist challenge (traditional ethics is biased against women) and (3) the multicultural challenge (traditional ethics is biased against non-Western cultures). Assuming some defensible form of ethics survives these challenges (again, you will have to determine whether that is the case), you should be in a much better position to make those ethical and moral choices that seem to force themselves upon our lives and to make them well. That is why you should read this book—it is designed to help you become a more ethical or moral person.

In contemporary moral and political philosophy, much work has been recently done to help resolve debates that have been raging among philosophers at least since the mid-1970s, and additional work has also been done to develop and reply to important challenges to traditional ethics from feminist, environmental, and multicultural perspectives. It is now appropriate to build on these successes and developments to write the kind of introductory ethics book that until now couldn't have been written.

Most importantly, this book strives to be relevant and accessible, especially to the newcomer to philosophy. Advances in ethics are of little use if they cannot be conveyed with relevant examples and accessible arguments. That is why the following examples and others are integrated into the arguments of this book to make them as accessible as possible to the reader: Osama bin Laden and 9/11, the Abraham and Isaac story from the Bible, animal experimentation, factory farming, alien species, female circumcision, the Hindu practice of suttee,

Ho Chi Minh and the Vietnam War, the Inuit practice of euthanasia, Bernard Madoff's Ponzi scheme, Andrew Jackson and the Trail of Tears, male/female gender roles, Nazi Germany under Hitler, the Sand Creek Massacre, the use of torture, the wage-gap in the United States, the traditional family, and the U.S. invasion of Iraq and the overthrow of Saddam Hussein.

So are you ready to improve your ability to make ethical or moral choices? Then keep reading!

GET CONNECTED WITH MYSEARCHLAB

Provided with this text, MySearchLab provides engaging experiences that personalize, stimulate, and measure student learning. Pearson's MyLabs deliver proven results from a trusted partner in helping students succeed.

Features available with this text include:

- A **complete eText**—Just like the printed text, you can highlight and add notes to the eText online or download it to your iPad.
- **Assessment**—chapter quizzes and flashcards offer and report directly to your grade book.
- **Writing and Research Assistance**—A wide range of writing, grammar, and research tools and access to a variety of academic journals, census data, Associated Press newsfeeds, and discipline-specific readings help you hone your writing and research skills.

MySearchLab can be packaged with this text at no additional cost—just order the ISBN on the back cover. Instructors can also request access to preview MySearchLab by contacting your local Pearson sales representative or visiting **www.mysearchlab.com.**

ACKNOWLEDGMENTS

I want to thank Oxford University Press, the University of Chicago Press, and Environmental Ethics for permission to reprint from my previous work.

Introduction

Ethics appears to be unlike other areas of inquiry. After all, we cannot find contemporary defenders of Ptolemy (AD c. 100–c. 170), Copernicus (1473–1543), or Isaac Newton (1642–1727), all claiming to have the best theory of the physics of celestial motion. Nor are there contemporary mercantilists or physiocrats, as there were in the eighteenth century, all claiming to have the best theory of macroeconomics. However, we can find contemporary defenders of Aristotle (384–322 BC), Immanuel Kant (1724–1804), and John Stuart Mill (1806–1873), for example, all claiming to have the best theory of ethics. While significant disagreements remain in other areas of inquiry, the extent of disagreement appears to be much greater in ethics.

Of course, one explanation for this seemingly greater disagreement in ethics is that there is little or nothing that can really be established in ethics. This would explain why so many of the ethical theories that have been proposed in the past continue to have their contemporary defenders. On this account, ethics simply lacks the resources to defeat any of the contending theories, and so they all remain live options. Obviously, this explanation does not put ethics in a very favorable light.

Fortunately, a better explanation is that traditional theories of ethics, be they Aristotelian, Kantian, Millian, or whatever, have come to be revised and reformed in such a way as to make them quite different from the original theories of the philosophers after whom they are still named. While Aristotle endorsed slavery and the subordination of women, and Kant advocated racism as well as the subordination of women, and Mill supported colonialism, it would be difficult to find any contemporary defenders of these philosophers who still endorse these particular views. Contemporary defenders all claim to be defending revised and reformed versions of Aristotle's, Kant's, and Mill's original ethical theories. So this would allow for progress to be made in ethics similar to the progress that has been made in other areas of knowledge. In this regard, then ethics would be like physics and economics.

WHY DO WE NEED THIS KNOWLEDGE?

Yet even if ethics is an area of inquiry where knowledge is advancing, why should we be concerned about acquiring the knowledge it offers? After all, there are many areas of knowledge that we, for good reason, choose not to learn about. Why should we choose to learn about ethics?

It is because ethics *is* still unlike many other areas of inquiry in one important respect. Valuable though many other areas of knowledge may be, most of us can live our lives quite well without acquiring many specialized types of knowledge, such as that of the physics of subatomic particles or macroeconomics. Ethics, however, is relevantly different from these other specialized types of knowledge that many of us can do without. As we noted in the preface, almost every day we make ethical choices. Sometimes even by failing to act, by failing to do something, we make ethical choices for which we subsequently can be held responsible. Given that we cannot avoid making ethical choices, surely it would be helpful to have the knowledge to make them the best we can.

Coming at the importance of ethics in a slightly different way, most of us like to think of ourselves as ethical and moral. To be truly such, however, we need to know about the demands of ethics or morality (which are used synonymously here) and how they apply in our own particular circumstances. Thus, we should be able to assess whether our society's economic and legal systems are just—that is, whether the ways income and wealth are distributed in society as well as the methods of enforcing that distribution give people what they deserve. We should also be able to assess whether other societal institutions, such as our defense system, our education system, and our foreign aid program, are truly just and moral. Without assessing these systems and coming to an informed judgment, we cannot say with any certainty that we are just and moral persons rather than the perpetrators or beneficiaries of injustice in our society.

Consider American Indian reservations in the United States. The destitution and ill health that prevails on many reservations today is similar to conditions in Third World countries:[1]

- On the Pine Ridge in South Dakota and Tohomo O'Odham in Arizona (where more than 60% of homes are without adequate plumbing, compared with 2% for the nation at large), the poverty rate is nearly five times the national average.
- On the Pine Ridge reservation, the average life expectancy is 50 years, compared to a 77.5 average life expectancy in the United States as a whole.
- On Pine Ridge, the teenage suicide rate is also 400% higher than the national average for the same age group, and the infant mortality rate is 500% higher than the national average.

Now how do we reconcile these facts about the Pine Ridge Reservation, in particular, with our claims to be just and moral? Could the distribution of income and wealth in the United States be just while these conditions still obtain on the Pine Ridge Reservation? If not, and if we happen to significantly benefit from the distribution of income and wealth in the United States, are we then not the beneficiaries, if not the perpetrators, of injustice?

Alternatively, suppose some of the Indians from the Pine Ridge Reservation showed up at your doorstep, or your dorm room asking for help. Could you justifiably turn them away, or would you be morally required to help them? Would it make any difference, and what difference would it make, if they just sent a letter to you asking for help? Would it make any difference, and what difference would it make, if those who showed up at your doorstep or sent a letter to you were from, say, somewhere in Bangladesh, rather than from the Pine Ridge Reservation?

Surely this example, like many others that could be given, points to the importance of the knowledge of ethics for those inevitable ethical choices that we make in our lives. Clearly, we need the kind of knowledge that this book purports to offer. So keep reading.

THREE CHALLENGES TO ETHICS

We must begin by taking up three challenges that deny that ethics itself can provide the kind of knowledge we have now convinced ourselves that we need for choosing well.

The first challenge comes from religion. This challenge denies that ethics itself provides an independent source of moral requirements. According to this view, the commands of God are the source of all moral requirements: Things are right or wrong simply on the basis of the commands of God. If this challenge is correct, ethics is subsumed by religion; it would have no independent status.

The second challenge, like the first, denies that ethics provides an independent source of moral requirements. However, this challenge comes from culture. It is the challenge of moral relativism. According to this view, culture is the source of all moral requirements; all moral requirements are simply the product of particular cultures and therefore are relative to and applicable to just the members of those particular cultures from which they arose. Ethics would have no independent status.

Egoism, the third challenge, goes beyond the other two and claims that there are no moral requirements, understood, as we normally understand them, to sometimes demand that we sacrifice ourselves for the good of others. The other two challenges did not deny the existence of moral requirements so understood. They just maintained that something else (religion in the one case, culture in the other) was the source of those requirements. Egoism, however, goes further and denies the very existence of moral requirements. It maintains that all we *can* do (psychological egoism) or all we *should* do (ethical egoism) is serve our own self-interest and not the interests of others. According to this view, ethics, as we normally think of it with its demand that we sometimes sacrifice ourselves for the good of others, is either a delusion (psychological egoism) or a scam (ethical egoism).

THREE TRADITIONAL ETHICAL PERSPECTIVES

If this book is successful at meeting the challenges of religion, moral relativism, and egoism, and so is able to establish that ethics provides us with an independent source of knowledge for making moral choices (you will have to determine for yourself whether this is the case), then it makes sense to go on, as the book does, to examine the three main traditional accounts of ethics as independent sources of knowledge that continue to have their contemporary defenders: utilitarian ethics, Kantian ethics, and Aristotelian ethics.

Utilitarian ethics requires us to always choose whatever action or social policy would have the best consequences for everyone concerned. Through a discussion of a wide range of examples from contemporary examples of torture and terror to hypothetical examples of spelunkers stuck in a cave with flood waters rising, the strengths and weaknesses of the view are considered. An effort is then made to evaluate the view under its most morally defensible interpretation.

Kantian ethics demands that we act in accord with a Categorical Imperative which in its first formulation requires us to act only on maxims that we can at the same time will to be universal laws. Again, a wide range of examples are used in an effort to provide the most morally defensible interpretation of Kant's view. Two influential interpretations of Kantian ethics—welfare liberalism and libertarianism—are then considered because they appear to provide the key to an ethical resolution to the Pine Ridge Reservation example.

Aristotelian ethics is presented as a way of *being* rather than as a way of *acting*. In this, it seems to contrast with both utilitarian and Kantian ethics. However, through the use of examples, an effort is made to bring the views, under their most morally defensible interpretations, closer together. Ayn Rand's attempt, through her essays and novels, to interpret Aristotelian ethics in a way that is strongly opposed to Kantian and utilitarian ethics is discussed in some detail because of its direct relevance to an ethical resolution to the Pine Ridge Reservation example.

The **Taking-Stock Interlude** then suggests that all three of these traditional ethical theories, when given their most morally defensible interpretation, seem to be leading to the same practical moral requirements. If this is the case, all we would need to do to improve upon our ability for making ethical choices is to use the theories to determine what their commonly endorsed practical moral requirements are.

But a problem remains. Traditional ethics—whether utilitarian, Kantian or Aristotelian—has itself been subject to challenges that it is morally defective. These challenges come from environmentalism, feminism, and multiculturalism. Clearly these challenges must be met if traditional ethics is to be useful—today and in the future—in helping us make morally defensible moral choices.

THREE MORE CHALLENGES TO ETHICS

The environmental, feminist, and multicultural challenges are significantly unlike the three challenges with which this book begins. The three challenges with which the book begins, those of religion, moral relativism, and egoism, all attempt to show that ethics is not an independent source of moral requirements (ethics is said to be based simply either on God's commands or on the requirements of particular cultures), or else to deny that there are any moral requirements at all (egoism). In contrast, the challenges of environmentalism, feminism, and multiculturalism are far friendlier to ethics. They do not want to undercut or deny ethics. Rather, their complaint is that traditional ethics needs to be morally improved upon to avoid bias. Specifically, the feminist challenge maintains that there is a masculine bias in traditional ethics and purports to show how to correct it, the environmental challenge maintains that there is a human bias in traditional ethics and purports to show how to correct it, while the multicultural challenge maintains that there is a Western bias in traditional ethics and purports to show how to correct it.[2]

Conclusion

If the challenges of environmentalism, feminism, and multiculturalism can be met (again, you will have to determine for yourself whether this is the case), then the common resources of utilitarian, Kantian, and Aristotelian ethics should be able to be put to good use in dealing with the ethical choices that we face in our lives. The final chapter of this book attempts to assess to what degree this is the case.

Notes

1. Stephanie M. Schwartz, "The Arrogance of Ignorance: Hidden Away, Out of Sight and Out of Mind," *Link Center Foundation* (2006), http://www.linkcenterfoundation. org/id24.html; David Stannard, *American Holocaust* (New York: Oxford University Press, 1992), 106, 256–7. More recent data suggest that poverty rates are even higher on the Pine Ridge Reservation.

2. This is not to deny that there have not been anticipations of these challenges within the traditional ethical perspectives, particularly utilitarian ethics where Jeremy Bentham, in a famous passage, raised the issue with respect to just sentient living beings, and John Stuart Mill, at the end of his life, published *The Subjugation of Women*. Unfortunately, these anticipations have not yet borne much fruit within the traditional views so that even today these challenges still remain outlier positions generally. This is the case even within utilitarian ethics, with the notable exception of Peter Singer on animal liberation.

CHAPTER 1

Religion and Morality

THE EUTHYPHRO QUESTION

In Plato's *Euthyphro*, Socrates raises a fundamental question for morality. We can put the question as follows:

- Are actions right because God commands them, or
- Does God command actions because they are right?

According to the first option, morality is fundamentally dependent on religion. According to the second, morality is fundamentally independent of religion in a way that even God, assuming there is a God, would have to affirm. In this dialogue, Socrates maneuvers Euthyphro into endorsing the second option, affirming that God commands actions because they are right, and hence, that morality is fundamentally independent of religion, an alternative that is still favored by many religious believers, and usually, but not always, by atheists and agnostics as well.[1] However, the first option—that actions are right because God commands them, and hence, that morality is fundamentally dependent on religion—also has its defenders. These defenders have been called "divine command theorists" because they identify morality simply with the commands of God.

To illustrate their view, divine command theorists often cite the following story from the Bible. In the book of Genesis, God tells Abraham, "Take your only son Isaac whom you love and go into the district of Moria and there offer him as a holocaust on a hill which I shall point out to you." Abraham did as he was told, but as he was about to sacrifice his son, an angel of the Lord stopped him by telling him, "I know now that you fear God, since you have not withheld your only son." And later he is told, "Since you have done this, and have not withheld your only son I will indeed bless you and will surely multiply your descendents as the stars of the heavens and sands of the seashore."[2]

In the story, Abraham does not argue with God, as he had done on an earlier occasion when God proposed to destroy Sodom and Gomorra. At that time, Abraham argued with God and got a reprieve for the cities on condition that "fifty just men" could be found in them. He went on to get the requirement of fifty reduced ultimately to just ten. In this way, Abraham does exhibit a willingness to argue with God.

With respect to God's command to sacrifice his son, however, Abraham does not argue with God at all. Rather, he immediately takes steps to do just what God commanded. In the end, Abraham is not required by God to make the ultimate sacrifice of his son; God is satisfied with Abraham's willingness to do what he was commanded to do, and for that God is said to have rewarded him handsomely.

The story of Abraham's near-sacrifice of his son has been taken to clearly illustrate divine command theory. It purports to show how an action that we might otherwise think is wrong—intentionally killing one's own innocent child—could be made the right thing to do if God commands it.

MEDIEVAL DEVELOPMENTS OF DIVINE COMMAND THEORY

During the Middle Ages, William of Ockham (1280–1349) explicitly extends this same divine command theory analysis to other actions:

> The hatred of God, theft, adultery, and actions similar to these actions ... can be performed meritoriously by an earthly pilgrim if they should come under divine precepts.[3]

In support of the same view, another medieval philosopher, Thomas Aquinas (1225–1274), offers the following explanation:

> Adultery is intercourse with another's wife, who is allotted to him by the law emanating from God. Consequently, intercourse with any woman by the command of God is neither adultery nor fornication. The same applies to theft, which is the taking of another's property. For whatever is taken by the command of God, to whom all things belong, is not taken against the will of its owner, whereas it is in that that theft consists.[4]

So what Ockham and Aquinas are saying here is that acts that previously were wrong, such as intentionally killing an innocent person (as in the case of Isaac), theft, adultery, even hatred of God, are transformed into acts that should be done if and when God commands that they be performed. This is because what made them wrong in the first place was that God commanded that they not be done. So if God were now to command differently with respect to them—command that they be done rather than that they not be done—then the moral character of the acts would change from being morally prohibited to being morally required.

MORALITY DEPENDENT ON GOD THROUGH CREATION

Divine command theorists want to show that morality is dependent on God, and so they argue that it depends simply on God's commands. But if one just wanted to show that morality is dependent on God, there is another approach that one could take that avoids endorsing divine command theory. All one needs to do is show that morality is dependent on our nature and the circumstances of our lives and, further, that our nature and circumstances are dependent on God through creation. In this way, morality would be dependent on God through being dependent on our nature and circumstances, which, in turn, are dependent on God through creation.

Seen in this way, God would also be able to change what humans ought to do, but it would have to be done by appropriately changing our nature or the circumstances of our lives. This is because without a change in our nature or circumstances, our capacities and opportunities would remain the same, and hence, a morality that depended on those capacities and opportunities would remain the same as well. If God were to appropriately change human nature or the circumstances of our lives, however, morality would then have to change correspondingly.

Thus, suppose that God were to change human nature such that if someone plunged a knife into a human being's heart, the person would die immediately, but then, spring back to life with great pleasure and no negative effects. Then, of course, we could see ourselves as having a new moral rule: Kill human beings by plunging a knife into their hearts as often as you can. Similarly, if God were to change the circumstances of our lives such that everything we needed was always in plentiful supply, the prohibition against theft could be seen to no longer apply to what we need. So God could be seen to change morality by appropriately changing human nature or the circumstances of our lives on which, from this perspective, our morality is based.

Yet divine command theorists have generally not been interested in arguing that morality is dependent on God because our nature and circumstances are dependent on God through creation. They want to claim that morality is dependent on God in a stronger sense such that the moral status of any significant act, such as intentionally killing an innocent person, adultery, fornication, or theft, can be changed by a command of God without presupposing any change in our nature or circumstances. On their view, all that are necessary to constitute a new and different morality are new and different commands of God.

PROBLEMS FOR DIVINE COMMAND THEORY

There are three significant problems for divine command theory that need to be addressed:

1. How are we to understand divine commands?
2. Can creation be used to justify divine command theory?
3. How are we to identify God's commands?

Let us examine each of these problems in turn.

How Are We to Understand God's Commands?

Suppose we had a list of God's commands, how should we understand them? We might think of God as a one-person legislature with ourselves having a role analogous to the judiciary and executive branches of government. God, as the one-person legislature, would make the commands/laws, and we, as the judiciary/executive, would have the task of interpreting and applying them.

There would be differences, however. The U.S. judiciary in interpreting the laws often tries to determine what purpose the legislature had in passing a particular law, and whether that purpose accords with the U.S. Constitution. And sometimes the U.S. judiciary strikes down laws passed by the legislature as unconstitutional.

According to divine command theory, however, there would be no comparable role for humans to have respect to the commands of God. We couldn't, for example, strike down any of God's commands because they failed to accord with some independent moral standard. Thus, our role in interpreting and applying God's commands under divine command theory would be narrowly circumscribed. Even so, there are further problems understanding what that role would be.

This is because divine commands could, presumably, come into conflict. Thus, suppose we had one divine command that we should each love and care for the members of our family and another that we should love and care for the deserving poor. Surely, these two commands would conflict when we are faced with the option of using our limited resources to either provide luxuries for the members of our family or use those same resources to provide for the basic needs of the deserving poor. Here we seem to require some kind of a background theory that compares the good that would be accomplished in each case as well as weighs the competing obligations involved, and then makes a recommendation about what should be done.

Yet divine command theory provides no such background theory for resolving conflicts between commands. Under the theory, each command is obligatory simply because it is commanded by God. Conflicts that arise among God's commands could be appropriately resolved only by another command of God that shows which command has priority. This is because, according to divine command theory, the resolution of conflicts always could go either way. So there is no way for us to figure out, in advance, how it should go. This then would leave us with only a very minimal role when interpreting or applying the commands of God, and in cases where those commands conflict, we would be at a complete loss as to what to do.

Are God's Commands Justified by Creation?

While divine command theorists do not base morality on human nature or the circumstances of our lives, they do want to appeal to the idea of God as Creator to justify their claim that there are no limits as to what sort of morality God could demand of us. As they see it, we have no other justifiable option but to do what God commands us to do, given that we are the product of God's labor. But if this argument from creation works, an analogous argument from procreation seemingly works as well.

The analogous argument from procreation is based on the fact that children are the products of their parents, particularly their mothers. A fertile woman, assuming she has been freely given a sperm, can make a baby using no other resources than her own body and its nourishment. The materials used in reproduction, an egg and a sperm, in themselves, are thought to be of little value, and when a women joins them together in her own body, the act of pro-creation looks like a paradigm case in which *making* creates a property right to what is made. But this would mean that a woman should own her children the way farmers own their produce, architects their blueprints, and artists their works of art. But at least today, a woman's act of reproduction is not thought to give rise to a property right to the child thereby produced. When what is produced is a human being, a person's productive labor is not thought to cre-ate an ownership right, the way it does in other contexts. Moreover, as human children grow to maturity, whatever guardianship rights their parents have over them are usually thought to diminish and ultimately disappear.

So why then should we think that, through an act of creation, God would derive unconditional and lasting rights over us when we don't recognize any analogous rights issuing from acts of procreation? Clearly, we do not think that acts of procreation give rise to property rights the way we do for other acts of human production. So why think that the act of creating human beings would have such different consequences from acts of procreating human beings?

What we really have here is a three-way comparison of divine creation, human procreation, and human production. Evaluating the three in terms of productivity, procreation is more similar to divine creation than it is to many acts of human production. Divine creation is making something valuable from nothing, while procreation is making something valuable from what has little value.[5] If productivity is primarily what gives rise to property rights to what is produced, then women should have stronger property rights over their off-spring than farmers should have over the bushels of corn they've produced. But if we don't draw this conclusion, it must be because we have judged that producing human beings does not give rise to property rights to what is pro-duced. But if this is true for human reproduction, it should be true for divine creation as well. Consequently, divine creation would not give rise to property rights either. What this shows is that the idea that we were created by God no more supports the prerogatives of divine command theory than human procre-ation supports property rights to the children whom are thereby produced.

How Are We to Identify God's Commands?

Another problem with divine command theory is determining what God has actually commanded us to do. It would seem that divine command theorists maintain that God's commands are received through special revelations to par-ticular individuals or groups. But if the commands of God are made known only to a few, how can others know what those commands are or when they are reasonably bound to obey them? Presumably, people can be morally bound only by commands they know about and have reason to accept.

To add a further complication, different individuals and groups have claimed to be recipients of different special revelations that conflict in ways which would support conflicting moral requirements. Of course, if some of those who claim to have received a special revelation rise to power, they may be able to force obedience on the rest. But then others would have no independent reason to go along with that forceful imposition.

RADICALLY MODIFIED DIVINE COMMAND THEORY

To deal with these problems of divine command theory, some theorists have distinguished between general and special revelations as sources of God's commands. According to Stephen Evans,

> [G]eneral revelation is the knowledge of God that God makes possible through observation of the natural world and through reflections on human experiences that are universal and commonly accessible.[6]

This is, of course, to recognize creation as a relatively independent source of moral requirements. Most importantly, it has the effect of radically modifying divine command theory. As the theory was originally formulated, moral requirements were determined simply by the commands of God. God could make anything right or wrong simply by commanding differently without making any change in our human nature or the circumstances of our lives.

Yet faced with conflicting special revelations, what else were divine command theorists to do? There was a clear need to appeal to a common ground to deal with apparently conflicting requirements of different special revelations. So that common ground was taken to be provided by normative requirements (i.e., the dos and don'ts) that are grounded in our nature and circumstances. It is also open for divine command theorists to claim that their favored special revelation provided the best interpretation of the normative requirements that are grounded in our nature and our circumstances. At the same time, atheists and agnostics can also accept the normative requirements that are grounded in our nature and circumstances as their sole basis for moral requirements. For the religious person, however, there remain two sources of morality:

- one being the normative requirements that are grounded in our nature and circumstances, or put another way, what can be known about the requirements of morality through reason alone,
- the other being what can be known about the requirements of morality through special revelation.

Hence, there still is the problem of what should be done if and when these two purported sources of morality come into conflict, especially, in the public arena.[7]

RELIGION AND THE PUBLIC ARENA

Attempting to deal with just that problem, contemporary philosopher John Rawls has argued that in the public arena, citizens should conduct their fundamental discussions within the framework of public reason, appealing only to reasons that others "can reasonably be expected to endorse."[8] Since all citizens in liberal, pluralistic societies, like our own, seemingly cannot reasonably be expected to share the same religious perspective, Rawls proposed that reliance on public reason generally rules out any role for religious considerations in public debate over fundamental issues in societies like our own.

Rawls further contends that normally citizens must be "able" and "ready" to explain to one another how the principles and policies they advocate and vote for can be supported by public reasons, or at least, they need to be prepared to do so in due course.[9] However, in the private arena, where our actions affect only ourselves or other consenting adults, Rawls would allow that no similar constraint on the use of purely religious reasons.

But is Rawls right about the need to exclude religious considerations from debate over fundamental issues in the public arena? Another contemporary philosopher Nicholas Wolterstorff argues that he is not. Wolterstorff writes:

> Is it equitable to ask of everyone that, in deciding and discussing political issues, they refrain from using their [religious] perspectives?...
>
> [This] seems to me not equitable. [For it] belongs to the religious convictions of a good many religious persons in our society that they ought to base their decisions concerning fundamental issues of justice on their religious convictions. They do not view it as an option whether or not to do so. It is their conviction that they ought to strive for wholeness, integrity, integration, in their lives; that they ought to allow the Word of God, the teachings of the Torah, the command and example of Jesus, or whatever, to shape their existence as a whole, including, then, their social and political existence. Their religion is not, for them, something else than their social and political existence; it is also about their social and political existence. Accordingly, to require of them that they not base their decisions and discussions concerning political issues on their religion is to infringe inequitably on their free exercise of their religion. If they have to make a choice, they will make their decisions about constitutional essentials and matters of basic justice on the basis of their religious convictions, and make their decisions on more peripheral matters on other grounds—exactly the opposite of what Rawls [recommends].[10]

Wolterstorff thinks he has provided another way of thinking about how the debate over fundamental issues in the public arena should proceed—one which lacks the unfairness that he believes characterizes Rawls's interpretation with its requirement of public reason.

Wolterstorff elaborates further on his view:

> In a democracy, we discuss and debate, with the aim of reaching agreement. We don't just mount the platform to tell our fellow citizens how we see things. We listen, and we try to persuade ... Seldom, even on unimportant issues, do we succeed in reaching consensus, not even among reasonable and rational citizens ... But we try.

Then, finally, we vote. It cannot be the case that in voting under these circumstances, we are violating those concepts of freedom and equality which are ingredient in the Idea of liberal democracy, since almost the first thing that happens when societies move toward becoming liberal democracies is that they begin taking votes on various matters and living with the will of the majority—subject to provisos specifying rights of minorities.

We aim at agreement in our discussions with each other.... Our agreement on some policy need not be based on some set of principles agreed on by all present and future citizens and rich enough to settle all important political issues. Sufficient if each citizen, for his or her own reasons, agrees on the policy today and tomorrow—not for all time. It need not even be the case that each and every citizen agrees to the policy. Sufficient if the agreement be the fairly-gained and fairly-executed agreement of the majority.[11]

So, according to Wolterstorff, debate over fundamental issues in the public arena has been conducted appropriately if, after all sides have had the opportunity to express their views, they abide by the results of majority voting, provided that the will of the majority is constrained by certain minority rights.

Wolterstorff contends that without the unfairness of Rawls's account of public reason, religious reasons will function more freely in public debate. Yet notice that Wolterstorff's interpretation of what it means for citizens to appropriately engage in public debate still constrains how religious reasons are to function in that debate. First, before religious reasons can be enacted in public policy, their advocates must muster a majority of the votes, and second, the enactment of such reasons is further constrained by minority rights, which Wolterstorff leaves unspecified here, beyond saying that Rawls's requirement of public reason should not be incorporated into these minority rights because it is unfair.

IS RAWLS'S REQUIREMENT OF PUBLIC REASON UNFAIR?

But is Rawls's requirement of public reason an unfair imposition on public debate? Let's grant that Wolterstorff has made a prima facie case that Rawls's requirement is unfair to religious majorities by limiting their use of religious reasons. What needs to be determined is whether this is the only unfairness at issue here. It would not do to correct one unfairness by imposing a similar or even greater unfairness. What we need to determine, therefore, is:

- whether a minority, religious or otherwise, that loses out to a religious majority might also be unfairly treated, and
- if it is unfairly treated, whether that unfairness needs to be addressed as much, or even more so, than the unfairness to which Wolterstorff has drawn our attention.

Presumably, if the imposition of the majority will on the minority is to be fair, it must be possible to morally blame the minority for failing to accept that imposition. If that were not the case, then the minority could justifiably resist that imposition, and the will of the majority would lack moral legitimacy.[12] But if the imposition of the will of the majority is to be fair, there must, then, be sufficient reasons accessible to the minority, religious or otherwise, that justify coercively requiring the minority to accept that imposition. For a group cannot be coercively required to do something if they cannot come to know and justifiably believe that they are so required.

For example, suppose a Christian majority decided to pass laws that severely taxed the rich to put into effect a preferential option for the poor they believed was demanded by the New Testament. If this were to happen, there would need to be reasons accessible to the wealthy non-Christian minority that are sufficient to justify coercively requiring their acceptance of the will of the majority on this issue. Such reasons would obtain, for example, if it were possible to show that a libertarian ideal of liberty that is usually taken to be opposed to a right to welfare actually requires that very right. If this derivation were widely known, it would serve the purpose of providing the minority in this case with the right sort of reason for going along with the Christian majority. In this way, the requirement of fairness would be met in this case.

Now Wolterstorff accepts this requirement of fairness; that is, he accepts the need for there to be reasons accessible to a minority that are sufficient to justify coercively requiring their acceptance of the will of the majority in the relevant cases. Moreover, Wolterstorff thinks that he has provided just the kind of reasons that are needed to produce that result. As he puts it, "It need not even be the case that each and every citizen agree to the policy. Sufficient if the agreement be the fairly-gained and fairly-executed agreement of the majority."[13] According to Wolterstorff, then, the fact that an agreement is fairly-gained and fairly-executed by a religious majority should provide the minority with sufficient reasons to morally justify coercively requiring its submission to the will of the majority. Moreover, such a fact should be accessible to a minority in a legitimate state, and its accessibility should make it unreasonable, and hence morally blameworthy, for the minority to fail to submit to the rule of the majority in such cases. Thus, by putting his justification for rule by a religious majority in terms of fairness, Wolterstorff must think that he is providing a moral justification that everyone in a liberal, pluralistic society should regard as sufficient to justify that rule.

Seeing Different Kinds of Unfairness

Yet Rawls and Wolterstorff may be disagreeing here because they are focused on different ways the public debate over fundamental issues may be unfair. Wolterstorff is clearly focusing on the unfairness of denying members of a religious majority the right to base their decisions on religious reasons, or the unfairness of requiring them to bifurcate their lives between what they are committed to religiously and what they are, or could be, committed to nonreligiously. Again, let us grant the prima facie unfairness of such requirements. Surely, fairness would:

1. Allow religious people to base their decisions on their religious reasons, provided that other requirements of fairness are satisfied.
2. Not require religious people to bifurcate themselves between what they are committed to for religious reasons and what they are committed to for nonreligious reasons, provided that other requirements of fairness are satisfied.

By contrast, Rawls is focusing on a different requirement of fairness for majority rule. He is focusing on the issue of whether minorities, whether religious or otherwise, would have sufficient reasons accessible to them for submitting to the rule of the majority. Wolterstorff appears to be aware of this problem, and that is why he put the case for rule by a religious majority in terms of an ideal of fairness. But fairness can have both procedural and substantive requirements. Fairness can procedurally require that a minority submit to a majority only after its members have had a chance to speak their minds and been outvoted.[14] But fairness can also substantively require that a minority submit to a majority when there are certain additional reasons that are accessible to the members of the minority that support the will of the majority by making it unreasonable, and hence morally blameworthy, for minority to fail to abide by the will of the majority. In the absence of such reasons, the majority would be simply imposing its preferences on the minority, which would be grossly unfair. This would be the case if, as we noted earlier, a Christian majority were to heavily tax the rich to implement a preferential option for the poor they found in the New Testament without, at the same time, having, for example, a widely available argument that shows that even a libertarian ideal of liberty, when correctly interpreted, supports a similar concern for the poor.

Now if a majority is only constrained procedurally, its impositions on a minority can turn out to be quite severe. For example, a religious majority could require a minority to financially support its religious activities or to participate in its religious services. The majority also, for example, could impose significant restrictions on women and on homosexuals as demanded by its religious doctrines. For example, in a concurring opinion of the South Dakota Supreme Court, Justice Frank Henderson denied a mother unsupervised overnight visits with her daughter, "[u]ntil such a time that she can establish after years of therapy and demonstrated conduct, that she is no longer a lesbian living a life of abomination (see Leviticus 18:22)."[15]

Moreover, such impositions typically would be much more constraining than the requirements that Rawls seeks to impose on public discourse. So, if fairness is to be secured, particularly with respect to questions of basic justice, there must be substantive reasons as well as procedural reasons that are accessible to the minority for accepting the will of the majority. And while these substantive reasons need not, by themselves, be sufficient to require abiding by the will of the majority, they must, when joined together with the procedural reasons that are also accessible to the minority, provide a sufficient justification to require abiding by the will of the majority. In Judge Henderson's case, statistical evidence would have to be put forward, showing that lesbian mothers are unlikely to be good parents to their children.

So it turns out that the requirements of fairness go further than Wolterstorff explicitly allowed. To meet the requirements of fairness, procedural reasons that are accessible to the minority are not enough; at least with respect to questions of basic justice, there must be substantive reasons that are also accessible to the minority, and taken together, these procedural and substantive reasons must constitute a sufficient justification to coercively require the minority to abide by the will of the majority by making it unreasonable, and hence morally blameworthy, for them to fail to abide by the will of the majority.

Of course, what the substantive reasons are that must be accessible to the minority to require its acceptance of the will of the majority vary to some degree from case to case. In general, however, imposing a set of constraints on majority rule modeled after the Bill of Rights and other amendments to the U.S. Constitution would make a significant contribution toward guaranteeing that the minority would have sufficient substantive reasons to accept the will of the majority.[16]

Nevertheless, it is necessary that this set of substantive constraints be interpreted as follows:

1. The right to free exercise of religion must be understood to be a sufficiently strong right such that no substantial burden should be placed on religious practice without a compelling state interest. For example, this right was violated by the U.S. Supreme Court's decision in *Employment Division v. Smith* (1990), which denied unemployment compensation to two state workers who were discharged for ingesting peyote for sacramental purposes at a ceremony of their Native American Church.[17]

2. The separation of church and state should not rule out the possibility of using public funds to equitably support both religious and public schools, provided a certain core curriculum is maintained and national educational standards are met. Here the U.S. Supreme Court seems to be slowly moving in this direction. In *Agostini v. Felton* (1997), the Court ruled that a federally funded program using government employees to provide remedial instruction on the premises of religious schools was not in violation of the Establishment Clause of the First Amendment to the U.S. Constitution.[18]

3. Equal protection must be interpreted such that it is strong enough to guarantee effective equal rights, particularly to those who are still held back by significant forms of discrimination, for example, African Americans, women, and homosexuals. A relevant U.S. Supreme Court decision in this regard was *Romer v. Evans* (1996), which struck down an amendment to the Colorado state constitution as discriminatory against homosexuals.[19]

CAN RELIGIOUS MORAL TEACHINGS BE REQUIRED BY REASON?

It might be objected, however, that although such constraints on majority rule have some merit, we don't really need them to provide the minority with a justification of the required sort for submitting to the will of the majority. All that is necessary, it might be argued, is that the majority simply seek to implement certain religious moral teachings, on the grounds that these religious moral teachings are accessible to virtually everyone in at least liberal, pluralistic societies,[20] which implies that everyone in such societies is able to understand that it is unreasonable to reject these teachings. For example, to assert that Christian moral teachings as such are accessible is to say that these teachings are accessible as part of a unique Christian salvation history, which has as key events, an Incarnation, a Redemptive Death, and a Resurrection.

Let us assess this objection. Surely, some religious moral teachings can be given a justification that is independent of the religion in which they are found (e.g., the story of the Good Samaritan[21])—a justification that is accessible to virtually everyone in at least liberal, pluralistic societies on the grounds that virtually everyone in such societies is able to understand that it would be unreasonable to reject those teachings so justified.[22] But the objection we are considering does not address the possibility of justifying religious moral teachings in this way. Rather, it claims that religious moral teachings are justified because, as such, they are accessible to virtually everyone in at least liberal, pluralistic societies, with the consequence that it would be unreasonable for virtually anyone in such societies to reject them.

But is this the case? Surely, for example, many Christian moral teachings are understandable to both Christians and non-Christians alike, but the sense of "accessible" we have been using implies more than this. It implies that persons can be morally blamed for failing to abide by such requirements because they can come to understand that these requirements apply to them and that it would be unreasonable for them to fail to abide by them. So understood, it would seem that Christian moral teachings as such are not accessible to everyone in liberal, pluralistic societies. Too many non-Christians, who seem otherwise moral, do not recognize the authority of Christian moral teachings as such, even though they may grant that some of these teachings have an independent justification. And the same would hold true here for non-Christian religious moral teachings as well.

Accordingly, religious moral teachings as such cannot serve as a substitute for accessible substantive reasons, like a set of constraints modeled somewhat after those found in the U.S. Constitution, which are needed, along with procedural reasons, to morally justify coercively requiring a minority to submit to the will of the majority. If the will of the majority is to be morally justified, there must always be accessible procedural and substantive reasons, which, taken together, constitute a sufficient justification to coercively require the minority to submit to the will of the majority.

HOW PUBLIC REASONS ARE TO BE MADE ACCESSIBLE

Nevertheless, fairness does not require that each and every advocate of the majority view be willing to offer these procedural and substantive reasons. While these reasons must be accessible to the minority, they can be accessible to the minority without requiring it to be the case that each and every majority advocate be able and willing to provide these reasons. For example, a particular member of a Hindu, Buddhist, Moslem, or Christian majority may think that his or her society should heavily tax the rich to provide for the poor without being able to provide an argument that is accessible to the minority that supports such a requirement, such as one grounded in a neutral ideal of liberty. So fairness does not impose on majority advocates the particular requirements that Rawls endorsed, requiring that each and every member of the majority be able and ready to explain the publicly accessible reasons for the policy they favor. Wolterstorff is correct in maintaining that such a requirement constitutes an unfair imposition on a religious majority.

Nevertheless, collectively, the majority does have an obligation to ensure that sufficient procedural and substantive reasons for going along with the majority are accessible to the minority, at least with respect to questions of basic justice. To meet this obligation, it generally suffices that the majority has taken sufficient steps to ensure freedom of speech, quality public education, and open debate for people of all persuasions. The idea is that, through these institutional structures, the needed public reasons will be made accessible. From time to time, however, this obligation will also require that some well-placed majority advocates help make accessible sufficient procedural and substantive reasons for the minority to go along with the will of the majority. By ensuring the accessibility to the minority of sufficient procedural and substantive reasons for their going along with the majority, this collective obligation of the majority is thereby discharged.

So what we have seen is that in the interests of fairness, we need to reject Rawls's requirement that each and every majority advocate be able to provide the minority in a society with sufficient reasons for going along with the will of the majority. It follows that much of the role that Wolterstorff and other critics of Rawls have wanted religious reasons to play in public debate can be justified. However, we have also seen that fairness requires that the minority be provided with more reasons accessible to them for accepting the will of the majority than the purely procedural reasons that Wolterstorff seems to favor. Additionally, both procedural and substantive reasons must be accessible to the minority, such that, when taken together, they are sufficient to require the minority's acceptance of the will of the majority. In addition, the majority has an obligation to ensure that such reasons are made accessible to the minority. In brief, we have seen that Rawls, his defenders, and his critics, like Wolterstorff, all have good reason to modify the practical requirements that they have endorsed in favor of requirements that are actually demanded by a requirement of fairness they all accept.

Conclusion

We started off this chapter with the central question that Socrates raises in Plato's Euthyphro: Are actions right because God commands them or does God command actions because they are right? We then pursued the answer given by divine command theorists that actions are right simply because God commands them. We saw how divine command theorists did not want to rely on the normative structure of human nature and the circumstances of our lives as a source of morality, but that they were then forced to do so because of the various problems facing their theory, most notably:

- the problem of conflicting requirements of different special revelations and
- the resulting need for some common normative ground provided by our nature and circumstances to help resolve those conflicts.

Yet there still was the problem of what to do if and when the requirements of the normative structure of our nature and circumstances come into conflict with the requirements of special revelation, particularly, in the public arena. Here we saw that fairness requires that there be sufficient reasons accessible to the minority to justify coercively requiring it to accept the will of the majority, but not that each and every member of that religious majority be willing and able to set forth such reasons. Nevertheless, the most important effect of the requirement of fairness in this regard is to limit the enforceability of religion to the part of it that can also be justified by the normative structure of our nature and the circumstances of our lives.

MySearchLab Connections

Watch. Listen. Explore. Read. MySearchLab is designed just for you. Each chapter features a customized study plan to help you learn key concepts and terms. Dynamic visual activities, videos, and readings found in the multimedia library will enhance your learning experience.

Here are a few questions and activities to help you understand this chapter:

1. How did Socrates "win" his argument with Euthyphro (p. 6)?

    📖 Read *Euthyphro*, MyPhilosophyLibrary.

2. What reasons did William of Ockham have for accepting divine command theory (p. 7)?

    📖 Read "William of Ockham," Multimedia Library, Web Resources, Internet Encyclopedia of Philosophy.

Each chapter features a customized study plan to help you learn and review key concepts and terms.

Notes

1. Some atheists and agnostics maintain with Nietzsche (1844–1900) that if there is no God (i.e., if God is dead), everything is permitted. And with this conclusion, divine command theorists seemingly agree.
2. Gen. 22 (Confraternity-Douay translation, 1963).
3. William of Ockham, "On the Four Books of the Sentences," from Book II Chapter 19, quoted and translated by Janice Idziak, *Divine Command Morality* (New York: Edwin Mellon Press, 1979), 55–56.
4. Thomas Aquinas, *Summa Theologica*, trans. the Fathers of the English Dominican Province (New York: Benziger Brothers), In First Part of the Second Part, Q96 A5 Reply to Obj. 2.
5. Even if one thought that God specially creates each human soul at conception, a mother would still produce her child's body or material substrate, which would be a very important productive contribution.
6. Stephen Evans, *Kierkegaard's Ethics of Love* (New York: Oxford University Press, 2004), 156.
7. In the private arena, a similar solution of conflicts can be reached without having to raise the question of whether the solution can be justifiably enforced.
8. John Rawls, *Political Liberalism* (New York: Columbia University Press, paperback edition 1996), 226. Throughout this discussion, it will be assumed that all citizens are morally competent, that is, sufficiently capable of understanding and acting upon moral requirements.
9. Ibid., 217–18 and li–lii.
10. Robert Audi and Nicolas Wolterstorff, *Religion in the Public Sphere* (Lanham: Rowman and Littlefield, 1997), 104–105.
11. Ibid., 108, 114.
12. The will of the majority if it is to be morally legitimate must be backed up with more than power. The minority must have a moral duty to accept the imposition of the majority, but that could be the case only if the minority would be morally blame-worthy for failing to accept that imposition. Moreover, as noted before (see n. 8), I am assuming throughout this discussion that everyone is morally competent, that is, sufficiently capable of understanding and acting upon moral requirements.
13. Audi and Wolterstorff, *Religion in the Public Sphere,* 114.
14. Except for his important provisos concerning minority rights, Wolterstorff might seem to be committed only to a procedural constraint on majority rule. But what if a majority decides to significantly limit the use of religious reasons in public debate (a possible trend of U.S. Constitutional history)? Would Wolterstorff rest content, or would he still object that such limitations are substantively unfair to the minority? It is likely that he would still object on grounds of substantive unfairness, and he would be right.
15. *Chicoine v. Chicoine,* 479 N.W. 2d 891 (1992).
16. Arguably, a right to welfare is another one of these constraining rights that should have same status as the U.S. Bill of Rights. See James P. Sterba, "The U.S. Constitution: A Fundamentally Flawed Document," in Christopher Gray, *The U.S. Constitution and its American Philosophers* (1989).

17. *Employment Division v. Smith*, 494 U.S. 872 (1990).
18. *Agostini v. Felton*, 65 U.S.L.W. 4524 (1997).
19. *Romer v. Evans*, 116 S.Ct. 1620 (1996).
20. The full scope of this accessibility claim would apply to anyone in any society who has been sufficiently exposed to Christian moral teachings as such.
21. Luke 10: 25–37.
22. The sense of "unreasonable" used here and normally throughout this book is moral, that is, to say that something is "unreasonable" is to say that it is "strongly opposed by moral reasons."

CHAPTER 2

The Challenge of Moral Relativism

Herodotus, the ancient Greek historian, tells a story about Darius the Great, King of Persia (550–486 BC), in support of moral relativism—the view that the requirements of morality are simply the product of a particular culture and therefore are relative to and applicable to just the members of that culture. In the story, Darius

> ... summoned the Greeks who happened to be present at his court and asked them what they would take to eat the dead bodies of their fathers. They replied that they would not do it for any money in the world. Later in the presence of the Greeks, and through an interpreter, he asked some Indians of the tribe called Callatiae, who do in fact eat their parents' [dead] bodies, what it would take to burn them. They uttered a cry of horror and forbade that he should even mention such a dreadful thing.[1]

Clearly, the Greeks and the Callatiae of Darius's time approved of their own particular way of showing respect for dead parents and disapproved the other's way of doing the same.

There are many other examples of this sort. Danish explorer Peter Freucher reports on the following practices of the Eskimos (Inuit) of the North in the early twentieth century:

> When an old man sees the young men go out hunting and cannot himself go along, he is sorry. When he has to ask other people for skins for his clothing, when he cannot ever again be the one to invite the neighbors to eat his game, life is of no value to him. Rheumatism and other ills may plague him and he wants to die. This has been done in different ways in different tribes, but everywhere it is held that if a man feels himself to be a nuisance, his love for his kin, coupled with the sorrow of not being able to take part in the things which are worthwhile, impels him to die. In some tribes, an old man wants his oldest son or favorite daughter to be the one to put the string around his neck and hoist him to his death.... Old

women may sometimes prefer to be stabbed with a dagger into the heart—a thing which is also done by a son or a daughter or whoever [*sic*] is available for the deed.[2]

Certainly, such practices toward the old are quite different from those that prevail in most Western societies today, and even different from the practices that now prevail among the Inuit. It is these and other such examples that are offered in support of the thesis of moral relativism—that the requirements of morality being the product of a particular culture are simply relative to and applicable to just the members of that culture.

NEGATIVE CONSEQUENCES FROM ENDORSING MORAL RELATIVISM

If we accept the thesis of moral relativism, we could never justifiably say that the cultural practices of other societies are morally inferior to our own. The authority of each society's moral code would extend no further than its own members.

For example, we could not blame Nazi Germany for the Holocaust in which 6 million Jews were killed. Nor could we condemn the North American colonists and, later, the citizens of the United States and Canada for the American Holocaust, which by 1890, together with the impact of European diseases, had reduced the North American Indian population by about 98 percent, to 381,000.[3] We also could not blame the Turks for the million Armenians they massacred or the Khmer Rouge for the million Cambodians who were massacred under Pol Pot's regime.[4] Obviously our inability to justifiably condemn any of these acts in the past or present is an undesirable consequence of accepting the thesis of moral relativism.

In accepting the thesis of moral relativism, there is also the problem of determining exactly what the requirements of morality are supposed to be relative to. It is said that they are relative to and a product of a particular cultural group. Yet must that group be a society as a whole, or could it be a subgroup of a society? And why can't morality be relative to each individual? Why can't moral requirements be determined just by each individual's own personal reflection and thereby be relative to and applicable to that individual alone? If we allow all of these possibilities, then, any act (e.g., contract killing) could be wrong from the point of view of some particular society (e.g., U.S. citizens), right from the point of view of some subgroup of that society (e.g., the Mafia), and wrong again from the point of view of some particular member of that society or other subgroup (e.g., law enforcement officers). But if this were the case, then obviously it would be extremely difficult for us to know what we should do, all things considered.

TOLERANCE—A BENEFIT FROM ENDORSING MORAL RELATIVISM?

Despite these negative consequences that follow from accepting moral relativism, some claim that accepting the view would have a positive consequence—greater tolerance among different cultural groups. According to the anthropologist Ruth Benedict, once moral relativism is widely recognized and embraced, we shall arrive at

> ... a more realistic social faith, accepting as grounds for hope and as new bases for tolerance the co-existing and equally valid patterns of life which mankind has created for itself from the raw materials of existence.[5]

Benedict is surely correct in claiming that if we all embraced moral relativism, we could not judge the actions and practices of those in other cultural groups as morally wrong or inferior to our own, using some culturally independent standard of evaluation. This is because, as moral relativists, we would not recognize any such culturally independent standard of moral evaluation.

Let us call this "judgmental tolerance" and grant that moral relativists would display this form of tolerance. But it does not follow that moral relativists would also be tolerant in their actions, and thus display "action-tolerance." Whether a particular cultural group displays action-tolerance depends on whether its cultural norms favor actions that conflict with the interests of other cultural groups. For example, if a particular group's cultural norms favor interference with or domination of other social groups, then the members of that group should not be expected to display action-tolerance.

Hoping to find a basis for greater tolerance in the practice of moral relativism, philosopher James Rachels has suggested that the normative requirements that a particular culture imposes on its members extend only to the borders of the country whose culture it is. For example, Rachels suggests that during World War II German soldiers entering Poland "became bound by the norms of Polish society—norms that obviously excluded the mass slaughter of innocent Poles."[6] But if Rachels's interpretation of moral relativism were correct, then, according to the view, countries could never justifiably seek to defeat an aggressor by carrying the war into the aggressor's own country. For example, during World War II, Allied forces could never justifiably have carried the war into Germany, Italy, or Japan.

Unfortunately, Rachels here confuses moral relativism's unwavering support for judgmental tolerance with support for action-tolerance. He fails to recognize that the view supports action-tolerance only when the cultural norms of a particular culture group do not conflict with the interests of other cultural groups. In the case of Nazi Germany, given that its cultural norms for expanding the German Fatherland clearly conflicted with the interest of Poles in maintaining an intact state, moral relativism would not have supported action-tolerance. If there were any moral relativists among the Nazis, they could just claim that while they were committed to judgmental tolerance—they did not judge the Poles to be morally inferior—they were not committed to showing them action-tolerance because their Nazi cultural norms required them to subjugate the Poles and other groups in the process of establishing the Third Reich. Judged from this relativistic point of view, of course, the Poles were perfectly free to try to stop the Nazis in their endeavor, insofar as they were able to do so—an option that unfortunately proved not to be of much help to the Poles. In brief, what this shows is that those who accept the thesis of moral relativism need not be very tolerant after all.

BUT IS IT TRUE?

Yet despite all the difficulties that come with accepting the thesis of moral relativism, the thesis might still be true.[7] So is there any way to reasonably determine whether the premise is true?

Consider the practice in the United States of driving on the right side of the road along with the opposite practice in the United Kingdom of driving on the left side of the road. What justifies these alternative practices? Well, in both countries, traffic must be regulated in some uniform way to avoid accidents, and each country adopted these different practices to secure that end. Accordingly, residents of each country can see the point of the other country's rule of the road, even though it differs from their own country's rule. In addition, residents of each country are normally willing to follow the other country's rule when they happen to be driving in that other country—"when in Rome do as the Romans do."

But are the different rules of the road in the United States and the United Kingdom an example of moral relativism? It is difficult to see how they could be. Surely, moral relativists must be maintaining that the requirements of morality are a product of the cultural practices of particular societies in some stronger sense than is displayed by our different rules-of-the-road example. There is too much moral agreement here about the purpose of the rules of the road and about what should be done in practice for this case to count as an example of moral relativism.

So let's consider the example of the ancient Greeks and the Callatiae with which we began this chapter. Here both groups presumably wanted to treat their dead respectfully, but they differed about how that should be done. Why did they differ? Most likely they had different religious beliefs about how best to show that respect. Religious belief, as we noted in Chapter 1, is grounded in special revelations and so is not rationally accessible to everyone. Accordingly, if the Greeks had realized this, they would have further realized that they should not have expected the Callatiae to accept their preferred religiously based way of caring for the dead. And the same would hold true for the Callatiae. They too should not have expected the Greeks to accept their preferred religiously based way of caring for the dead. Since in this context there is no necessity that they all care for their dead in exactly the same way, what both groups should have wanted is for each to be free to respectfully care for their dead in whatever way they prefer. This is because the moral requirement to respectfully care for the dead leaves open the means by which that requirement is to be satisfied, thus making it possible for different religious beliefs to enter into the determination of how to meet that same moral requirement. So here too the relativity exhibited in this example is not the right sort needed to show that the thesis of moral relativism is true. The example is too similar to the alternative-rules-of-the-road example for it to support moral relativism.

What about the example drawn from the practices of Inuit of the early twentieth century? At first glance, it does seem like we today hold different moral views about how the elderly should behave. Nevertheless, in Western cultural traditions, we find many examples of individuals who have become a burden on the group showing a willingness to sacrifice themselves to increase the chances that others will survive. In the early twentieth century, in a similar environment, such behavior was displayed by members of the British expedition attempting to reach the South Pole led by Sir Ernest Shackleton, and even more generally, such behavior can be found throughout the history of European and American warfare.[8] We also find that among the Inuit of today, with better means of survival, the elderly no longer engage in their earlier practice. So instead of viewing this case as one where different moral beliefs are simply the product of different cultures, it is better interpreted as a case where the same moral requirements are instantiated differently because of the presence of different opportunities and different material conditions.

In sum, in none of these cases are the moral requirements involved simply the product of the particular culture. Rather, they are cases in which the same moral requirements are, for appropriate reasons, met differently:

- In the first case, American and British drivers are in complete agreement about the purpose and application of a rule of the road.
- In the second case, the moral requirement to respect one's dead is met differently by the Greeks and the Callatiae because of different religious beliefs.
- In the third case, the moral requirements pertaining to Inuit self-sacrifice, especially when one is a burden to others, are met differently because of different opportunities and different material conditions.

Yet not all purported examples of moral relativism are like the ones we have just considered. Take a look at the following three examples:

Rape and Marriage

In 1965, Franca Viola from Alcomo, Sicily, "broke a thousand years of Sicilian tradition" by refusing to marry a rich man's son after the son had raped her. This son, Filippo Melodia, having failed as a suitor, kidnapped Viola and raped her with the expectation that she would then marry him to avoid the loss of honor to herself and her family that would otherwise result if she were to refuse. But Viola did refuse, and with the support of her father, she brought charges against Melodia and the other men who assisted him in the kidnapping. Viola and her family were intimidated and ostracized by most of the townspeople. Her father received death threats and their barn and vineyard were burned to the ground. But Viola prevailed against Melodia and his accomplices in the trial. Melodia was sentenced to ten years in prison. Viola later married her childhood sweetheart, who on the day of their wedding carried a gun for protection.[9]

Widows and Suttee

In 1987 an exceptionally beautiful and relatively well-educated eighteen-year-old named Roop Kanwan from Deorala, India, mounted her husband's funeral pyre and was burned to death. Her husband had died suddenly from an appendicitis after only eight months of marriage. She now faced the prospect of spending the rest of her life as a childless widow who could never remarry. She was expected to shave her head, sleep on the floor, wear only simple white clothes, and perform menial tasks. The next morning following her husband's death, Kanwan, dressed in her finest wedding sari, led about five hundred of the villagers to the cremation site. With Brahman priests looking on, offering prayers, Kanwar climbed on to the funeral pyre next to her husband's body, laying his head on her lap. She then signaled her brother-in-law to light the kindling. Within half an hour, Kanwar and her husband were reduced to ashes in accord with the ancient custom of suttee. In the fortnight following her death, 750,000 people had turned up to worship at the site of her pyre. Thirty-seven villagers were later charged with murder, but after nine years of legal proceedings, all were cleared of the charge. Nevertheless, some claimed that her in-laws pressured her into the suttee and drugged her with opium. And one unnamed farmer, quoted in a Bombay newspaper, said that she tried to get off the pyre three times and was pushed back onto it by irate villagers.[10]

Female Circumcision: A Personal Account

"I will never forget the day of my circumcision which took place forty years ago. I was six years old. One morning during my school summer vacation, my mother told me that I had to go with her to her sisters' house and then to visit a sick relative.... We did go to my aunts' house and from there all of us went straight to [a] red brick house [I had never seen].

"While my mother was knocking, I tried to pronounce the name on the door. Soon enough I realized that it was Hajja Alamin's house. She was the midwife who performed circumcisions on girls in my neighborhood. I was petrified and tried to break loose. But I was captured and subdued by my mother and two aunts. They began to tell me that the midwife was going to purify me ...

"The women ordered me to lie down on a bed [made of ropes] that had a hole in the middle. They held me tight while the midwife started to cut my flesh without anesthetics. I screamed till I lost my voice.... After the job was done, I could not eat, drink or even pass urine for three days. I remember that one of my uncles who had discovered what they did to me threatened to press charges against his sisters. They were afraid of him and they decided to bring me back to the midwife. In her sternest voice she ordered me to squat on the floor and urinate. It seemed like the most difficult thing to do at that point, but I did it. I urinated for a long time and shivered with pain.

"I understood the motives of my mother, that she wanted me to be clean, but I suffered a lot."[11]

In these three cases, unlike our previous examples, the disagreement about what should be done seems to be more fundamental, and there does not seem to be any agreement about basic moral requirements that lie behind these disagreements. Do these examples, then, support the thesis of moral relativism? Do these examples show that the requirements of morality are simply the product of a particular culture and therefore are relative to and applicable to just the members of that culture? Let us examine each in turn to determine whether this is the case.

Analysis of the Case of Rape and Marriage

In the first case, Franca Viola and her rejected suitor, Filippo Melodia, fundamentally disagree about what each of them should or is permitted to do. Yet in order for this disagreement to support the thesis of moral relativism, it must be grounded in a disagreement over moral requirements or entitlements. This means that in the Sicilian society of his time, Melodia must have been thought to be morally entitled to rape the woman he sought to marry in order to get her to consent to marry him, and Viola, after she was raped, must have been thought to be morally required to marry him. This contrasts, of course, with what obtains in virtually all Western societies today and even with what obtained in the particular subgroup to which Viola belonged in her day, where rejected suitors were thought to have no such moral entitlements and victims of rape no such moral requirements.

Yet while Viola and Melodia disagree, it is not over moral entitlements and moral requirements. Clearly, individuals or groups can disagree without their disagreement being a moral one. So let's see if we can determine, in general, when a disagreement over entitlements and requirements is specifically a moral one, first in the case of individuals and then in the case of groups.

In the case of individuals, thinking something is morally right is different from just thinking that you ought to do that thing. You could think that you ought to do something from a purely selfish standpoint. That clearly would be different from thinking that you morally ought to do something. To think that you morally ought to do something, you would need to appropriately take the interests of others into account. But in doing so, you need not regard them of equal weight to your own. You could favor your own interests, particularly your basic interests, over the interests, even over the basic interests, of others, in such an appropriate weighing. Nevertheless, in such a moral weighing, it would be inappropriate to prefer your own nonbasic interests over the basic interests of others by aggressing against their basic needs to satisfy your own nonbasic or luxury needs. Of course, this only roughly characterizes the sort of deliberation that must at least implicitly be involved when forming a judgment of what you morally ought to do. But without this sort of deliberation being at least implicitly involved, the resulting judgment of what you ought to be cannot justifiably be regarded as a moral one.[12]

Taking this into account, what can we say about Melodia's decision to rape Viola to get her to marry him? Did he reach his decision by appropriately weighing his own relevant interests against the relevant interests of Viola and then reaching the conclusion that he morally ought to rape Viola? It seems very unlikely that Melodia did anything of the sort. At best, he relied on the authority of his cultural group to which he belonged to justify his actions. Of course, that may be sufficient if the relevant culture group—Sicilian society as a whole—had already appropriately determined that the norms on which Melodia relied were moral ones.

That fact brings us to our second question: When are the entitlements and requirements recognized by a social group appropriately determined to be moral ones? More specifically, how could a social group justifiably come to the conclusion that someone in Melodia's situation is morally entitled to rape Viola to get her to marry him and that someone in Viola's situation is morally required to marry Melodia after he has raped her? Surely the group would have to deliberate in an appropriate way to justifiably determine what individuals like Melodia and Viola are morally entitled or required to do in these circumstances. This would require the group to replicate to some degree the same sort of deliberation that we imagined an individual going through when she justifiably reached a judgment about what she morally ought to do. It would thus involve giving appropriate weight to the interests of the different individuals and subgroups in the larger social group.

It would help to do this if those with conflicting interests were in communication with one another so that they could explain the importance of their interests and hear from one another an account of the importance of their interests as well. There would also be the need to ensure adequate representation for the interests of those who are incapable, or poorly situated, to represent themselves. Then there would be a need for a fair weighing of the conflicting interests involved, taking into account the relative importance of the interests of different individuals and subgroups.

Now the laws of a particular society are frequently put forward as an approximation of just such a moral weighing of the relevant conflicting interests in a society, at least insofar the resolution of those conflicts requires coercive enforcement. Even so, the laws and customs of particular societies can and do fall short of an adequate moral weighing of the relevant conflicting interests. And, at its worst, the legal system may pay only lip service to achieving that goal. When this happens, the laws and customs of a particular society are not morally justified. Hence, they do not reflect the moral entitlements and requirements that people are bound to observe.

Of course, people sincerely trying to be moral may still observe such laws, and may even try to get others to observe them as well. This is because doing anything else is likely to turn out to be even more costly to those whose interests have already been unjustly treated by the legal system. In so acting, however, they would in no way be conferring moral legitimacy on the oppressive legal system under which they are living. They would also be looking for opportunities to open up to reform or drastically change that unjust legal system as opportunities present themselves.

Applying these considerations to an evaluation of whether the norms and laws of Sicilian society on which Melodia relied, it is fairly obvious that they fell far short of adequately taking Viola's interests into account. Viola's interests in not having to marry a man she rejected who had then raped her were not fairly weighed against Melodia's interests in marrying whomever he wanted according to the laws and customs of Sicilian society at that time. Therefore, the laws and customs of Sicilian society at that time did not constitute or reflect the relevant moral entitlements and requirements in this case, and so the conflict between Melodia and Viola is not one of two people committed to different moral entitlements and requirements. In fact, only the entitlements and requirements that Viola supported in this case had any claim to be moral at all. Hence, this case does not provide the sort of conflict that is needed to support the thesis of moral relativism.

Analysis of the Case of Widows and Suttee

The case of Roop Kanwan's act of suttee presents a different problem for any attempt to use it to support the thesis of moral relativism. The problem is that the principal grounds offered to justify her action are simply religious, and thus lack any independent moral justification. According to Hindu religious tradition, when a husband's death preceded that of his wife, she was responsible for his death either because of a sin in this life or a previous one. As a consequence, only two alternatives were open to her. She could choose suttee and then she, her husband, her husband's family, her mother's family, and her father's family would be in paradise for 35 million years no matter how sinful any of them had been.[13] Alternatively, she could live the rest of her life out as a penitent sinner, eating no more than one very plain meal a day, performing the most menial tasks, never sleeping in a bed, wearing nothing but the drabbest clothes, and having her hair shaved monthly by an untouchable male barber. Such behavior was said to be required for the sake of her husband's soul and to keep herself from being reborn as a female animal.[14] Nevertheless, a religious justification, unless supplemented by an independent moral justification, cannot generate the sort of conflict that is needed to support the thesis of moral relativism. Moral relativism requires conflicting moral perspectives.

Still, there is a moral dimension to the choice Kanwan faced. This is because rather than allowing her the freedom to practice or not practice her religion, the laws and norms of her community forced her to choose between an act of suttee and an austere life as a widow. She lacked the option of not living the austere life prescribed for widows who choose not to commit suttee. The laws of property and employment in her society precluded any such third option. However, as we saw in Chapter 1, coercing people on religious grounds alone is morally objectionable. So what we have here is not a conflict between two moral perspectives. Rather, we have a religious perspective that lacked a moral justification for its coercive enforcement of very limited options on widows. As such, this is not the kind of case that is needed to support the thesis of moral relativism.

Analysis of the Case of Female Circumcision

With respect to the case of female circumcision, the following considerations are relevant to determining whether the practice supports the thesis of moral relativism.

First, there are basically three different types of female circumcision:

1. Clitoridectomy, the partial or total removal of clitoris,
2. Excision, the partial or total removal of both the clitoris and the outer labia (the outer labia are "the lips" surrounding the vagina), and
3. Infibulation, the narrowing of the vaginal opening through the creation of a covering seal by cutting and repositioning the inner, and sometimes outer, labia, with or without removal of the clitoris, leaving an opening that may be as small as a matchstick for the passage of urine and menstrual blood.[15]

Second, we must consider the medical consequences of the practice. Generally performed under unsanitary conditions and without anesthesia (as in our example), it can lead to potentially fatal complications, such as hemorrhage, infection, and shock. The inability to pass urine because of pain, swelling, and inflammation following the operation may lead to urinary tract infections. Infibulation is particularly likely to cause long-term health problems. Because the urethral opening is covered, repeated urinary tract infections are common. If the opening is very small, menstrual flow may be blocked, leading to reproductive tract infections and lowered fertility or sterility. In addition, the amputation of the clitoris and other sensitive tissue can reduce a woman's ability to experience sexual pleasure. Some studies, however, show that a high percentage of women with all three forms of circumcision still experience orgasms during their marriages.[16] For infibulated women, the consummation of marriage is likely to be painful because of the small vaginal opening and the lack of elasticity in the scar tissue that forms it. Tearing and bleeding may occur, or the infibulation scar may have to be cut open to allow for penetration. To allow for childbirth, the infibulation scar may have to be cut even more and then resewn many times during the woman's reproductive years.[17]

Third, there are three main justifications offered for performing the various forms of female circumcision on girls from infancy to fifteen:

1. It reduces women's sexual pleasure and thus helps them to resist illicit acts.[18]
2. It safeguards a girl's virginity considered essential to her family's ability to arrange her marriage and receive a brideprice, as well as to family honor. (In Somalia, a bride's body may be inspected by a prospective husband's family prior to marriage, and infibulated daughters are regularly checked by their mothers to ensure that they are still "closed.")[19]
3. It is expected that a woman be circumcised in some form or other to be eligible for marriage.[20]

But do these "justifications" constitute a moral justification for female circumcision?

In order for that to be the case, these justifications would be the outcome of a fair evaluation of the interests of men and women, boys and girls. But do these justifications embody such fairness? Consider this question: If it is good to use female circumcision to reduce women's sexual desire and help them to resist illicit acts, why shouldn't something comparable be done to men, like putting some kind of a restraining clamp on men's penises? Actually, it turns out, something comparable is being done to men, although not intentionally, but as the unforeseen consequence of actions that are undertaken for other purposes.

Here are the facts. About 12 million males are circumcised annually (compared to 2 million females). In the United States 79 percent of adult men have been circumcised. While male circumcision usually involves just removing the foreskin of the penis, we now know that the foreskin contains the greatest concentrations of nerve endings.[21] Its removal, therefore, should, as with the removal of a woman's clitoris, similarly be expected to reduce male capacity for sexual pleasure. Yet reducing sexual pleasure, and thereby decreasing men's desire for it, is surely not the reason that is usually given for the practice. In fact, if this likely effect of the practice of male circumcision were more generally known, we might reasonably expect a steep decline in the practice. So the basic unfairness remains: intentionally imposing the burden of circumcision on women in order to reduce their sexual desire and thereby help them resist illicit acts while not intentionally imposing any comparable burden on men to achieve that same effect.

The second reason for female circumcision applies only to the third form of female circumcision (infibulation) and that accounts for only 10 percent of female circumcisions. But in order for this drastic step to ensure female purity (virginity before marriage, fidelity after it) to be morally justified, a comparably drastic step would need to be taken to ensure male purity as well. (You can let your imagination go here as to what such a step might be.) Of course, this is not to say that infibulation would be morally justified if a comparable drastic step were taken to ensure male purity. It is just that without the burden of a comparable practice being imposed on men, imposing the burden of this practice on women cannot even begin to be morally justified.

In contrast, with the first and second justifications for female circumcision, the third justification does have considerable force in places where the practice is widespread. This is because when the practice is widespread, it can be difficult for families not to circumcise their daughters. Not to circumcise reduces their daughter's prospects for marriage in a context where the prospects for unmarried women in the society are even more undesirable. Accordingly, if undergoing some form of circumcision is expected for a woman to be an eligible marriage partner (some countries have female circumcision rates of between 94 and 98 percent[22]), a woman who is not circumcised can be at an enormous disadvantage. Thus, you can understand the willingness of parents to circumcise their daughters in such societies, because the consequences of not doing so are so much worse.

The actions taken here are analogous to those taken by people attempting to cope with other unjust laws in their societies. Sometimes people will have no real option but to obey those unjust laws themselves and get others to do so as well, because the consequences of not doing so for all concerned would be far worse. Even so, while going along with such unjust laws or practices, there is a need to constantly be on the lookout for ways to evade, reform, or drastically change those laws or practices whenever possible.

Nevertheless, the willingness of good people to go along with the practice of female circumcision under unjust conditions because the consequences of not doing so are far worse does not provide a moral justification for the practice, and hence the conflict that individuals and groups experience with respect to the practice cannot, therefore, be used to support the thesis of moral relativism.

A COMPARISON TO DIVINE COMMAND THEORY

It might be useful here to note the way in which moral relativism is like divine command theory, as discussed in Chapter 1. Divine command theory identifies morality with what God commands independently of what the facts about our nature and the circumstances of our lives happen to be—anything can be made right or wrong by the command of God. Moral relativism similarly identifies morality with what accords with the societal cultural norms no matter what the facts about our nature and of the circumstances of our lives happen to be, no matter what the impact those norms have on the interests of particular individuals.

In both cases, we can respond that morality, correctly understood, is a way of thinking that requires that the facts about our nature and circumstances be fairly taken into account. It thereby constrains both what God could legitimately command and what societal norms could legitimately require.

THE STANDARD CRITICISM OF MORAL RELATIVISM

As it turns out, most critics of moral relativism see the view as starting out with a descriptive thesis—that people in different societies disagree radically with respect to their moral beliefs. They then interpret the view to be using this descriptive thesis to support what we have been calling the thesis of moral relativism.[23] Let's now call our thesis—that the requirements of morality are simply the product of a particular culture and therefore are relative to and applicable to just the members of that culture—the relativity thesis. What these critics have then done—it is their main critique of moral relativism—is to argue that the relativity thesis does not follow from the descriptive thesis. From the fact that people in different cultures have different moral beliefs (the descriptive thesis), it does not logically follow that the requirements of morality are simply the product of a particular culture and therefore are relative to and applicable only to the members of that culture (the relativity thesis). This does not logically follow because where such conflicts exist, the moral beliefs of the members of one or the other society could be shown to be morally preferable. Because of that possibility, these critics claim, the argument from the descriptive thesis to the relativity thesis fails.

Now while this critique of moral relativism has some merit, what the discussion of our last three examples, in particular, has shown is that this standard critique of relativism concedes too much to the defenders of the view. What it concedes is that both sides have been thinking morally about the matter and, sadly, each has come up with conflicting moral beliefs. By contrast, what the analysis here shows is that when we look very carefully at the proposed cases, we don't find that all sides have been thinking morally about the conflicts, and hence, the conflicts that characterize the cases are not moral ones.

OUR SIX PURPORTED CASES OF MORAL RELATIVISM

So, let's review the analyses of the six cases we have been looking at:

1. *The different rules of the road in the United States and the United Kingdom.* Analysis: There is too much moral agreement here about the purpose of the rules of the road and about what should be done in practice for this case to count as an example of moral conflict.

2. *The different ways of caring for their dead of the ancient Greeks and the Callatiae.* Analysis: Both groups presumably wanted to treat their dead respectfully. Their behavior was grounded in the same moral belief. They should have also recognized that since morality does not establish one way to do that, the groups can legitimately use their different religious beliefs to specify what they should do. There is no moral conflict in this case.

3. *The different ways Inuit elderly of the early twentieth century behaved and the ways our elderly and the Inuit elderly of today behave.* Analysis: The same moral requirements pertaining to self-sacrifice, especially when one is a burden to others, seem to be met differently in these different historical periods because of different opportunities and different material conditions. Hence, there is no moral conflict between what they did and what is done today.

4. *The different views of Filippo Melodia and Franca Viola concerning the legitimacy and proper response to the rape and subsequent marriage proposal of a rejected suitor.* Analysis: Melodia and the Sicilian society on which he relied failed to do a fair evaluation of the competing interests involved in this case. Only Viola and those who supported her came up with and acted upon a fair evaluation of the competing interests. There was no moral conflict about what should be done.

5. *The different views over whether Roop Kanwan should have burned herself to death in an act of suttee.* Analysis: The only justification available for Kanwan's act is religious, so there cannot be conflicting moral views concerning whether she should have performed the act. However, the way in which her alternatives to engaging in suttee were limited was morally objectionable.

6. *Different views over whether female circumcision should be practiced.* Analysis: The justifications offered for the practice do not meet the requirements for a moral justification. In an unjust society, where the practice is widespread, however, there is a moral justification for currently going along with the practice to avoid even worse consequences. But this does not constitute a moral justification for the practice. The practice does not have a moral justification. Nor is it clear how the practice could be modified by creating a parallel practice for men so that it could then be morally justified.

Conclusion

Summarizing our six examples, we have failed to uncover any case that supports the thesis of moral relativism—the view that the requirements of morality are simply the product of a particular culture and therefore are relative to and applicable to only the members of that culture. To support this thesis, what we needed to find are cases of moral conflict grounded in cultural conflict. What we found in three of our six cases is far too much agreement to be cases of moral conflict. In the other three cases, we did find significant disagreement, but not the kind of disagreement that could be characterized as moral conflict.[24] This left the thesis of moral relativism unsupported.

To completely defeat the view, however, we must do more than defeat examples that purport to support the thesis of moral relativism. To completely defeat the view, what we need is a positive defense of a nonrelativist morality. Happily, just such a defense is proposed at the end of Chapter 3.

MySearchLab Connections

Watch. Listen. Explore. Read. MySearchLab is designed just for you. Each chapter features a customized study plan to help you learn key concepts and terms. Dynamic visual activities, videos, and readings found in the multimedia library will enhance your learning experience.

Here are a few questions and activities to help you understand this chapter:

1. What does moral relativism have in common with other forms of relativism (p. 23)?

    Read "Relativism," Multimedia Library, Web Resources, Internet Encyclopedia of Philosophy.

2. What contributions have anthropologists made to the discussion of moral relativism (pp. 23–24)?

    Read "Moral Relativism," Multimedia Library, Web Resources, Stanford Encyclopedia of Philosophy.

Each chapter features a customized study plan to help you learn and review key concepts and terms.

Notes

1. Herodotus, *The Histories*, trans. Aubrey de Selincourt, rev. A. R. Burn (Harmondsworth, Middlesex: Penguin Book, 1972), 219–20.
2. Peter Freuchen, *Book of the Eskimos*, ed. Dagmar Freuchen (Cleveland: The World Publishing Co., 1961), 194–5.

3. See David Stannard, *American Holocaust* (New York: Oxford University Press, 1992) and Leonre Stiffarm with Phil Lance, Jr. "The Demography of Native North America," in *The State of Native America*, ed. Annette Jaimes (Boston: South End, 1992), 36.

4. See Benjamin Valentino, *Final Solutions* (Ithaca: Cornell University Press, 2005).

5. Ruth Benedict, *Patterns of Culture* (London: George Routledge, 1983), 201.

6. James Rachels and Stuart Rachels, *The Elements of Moral Philosophy*, 6th ed. (New York: McGraw-Hill, 2010), 17.

7. Sometimes the thesis of moral relativism is objected to on the grounds that it is self-contradictory because while the thesis claims that morality should be understood relativistically, the thesis itself is taken to be a nonrelativistic claim supposedly true at all times and places. Yet while the thesis of moral relativism does maintain the relativity of the truth of moral claims, the thesis itself is not understood to be a moral claim. Rather, it is understood to be a meta-claim about moral claims. For this reason, it does not follow that what the thesis claims is true of moral claims is true of itself. Still, we might wonder why we should understand one class of claims relativistically but not another.

8. See Ernest Shackleton, *South* (Guilford, CT: The Lyons Press, 1998).

9. Dierdre Viola, Franca Viola, *The Florentine Issue* 78, April 30, 2008; John W. Cook, *Morality and Cultural Differences* (New York: Oxford University Press, 1999), 35.

10. William Dalrymple, *The Survival of Suttee*, 44 (1997), 16–17.

11. From a 1989 interview with Aisha Abdel Majid, a Sudanese woman working as a teacher in the Middle East. Quoted in Rogaia Mustafa Abusharaf, "Unmasking Tradition," *The Sciences* (March/April, 1998): 23.

12. Of course, we could define morality so that it allows the interests of some to be basically ignored by its requirements. But this is not how we normally understand morality, and the "moral conflict" needed to support the thesis of moral relativism would simply be a consequence of using this unusual definition of morality. Moreover, there is nothing to recommend this approach.

13. Dorothy Stein, "Women to Burn: Suttee as a Normative Institution," *Signs* 4, no. 2 (1978): 255–6.

14. Ibid.

15. WHO, "Female Genital Mutilation," http://www.who.int/mediacentre/factsheets/fs241/en/index.html.

16. Elizabeth Heger Boyle, *Female Genital Cutting: Cultural Conflict in the Global Community* (Baltimore: The Johns Hopkins University Press, 2002), 60ff.

17. Frances Althaus, "Female Circumcision: Rite of Passage or Violation of Rights," *International Family Planning Perspectives* 23, no. 3 (September 1997): 3.

18. WHO, "Female Genital Mutilation."

19. Althaus, "Female Circumcision: Rite of Passage or Violation of Rights," 4.

20. WHO, "Female Genital Mutilation."

21. Robert Darby and Steven Svoboda, "A Rose by Any Other Name? Rethinking the Similarities and Differences Between Male and Female Genital Cutting," *Medical Anthropology Quarterly* 21, no. 3 (2007): 301–323.

22. Althaus, "Female Circumcision: Rite of Passage or Violation of Rights," 2.

23. This trivial descriptive thesis is frequently called the thesis of cultural relativism.

24. Of course, there are cases of moral conflict, like the conflict over the abortion question, where each side claims that the other either is wrong or lacks a conclusive argument for its position. In these cases, however, neither side thinks the morality of the issue is simply relative to cultural norms.

CHAPTER 3

The Challenge of Egoism

Plato's *The Republic* (c. 380 BC) recounts a story about Gyges, a shepherd in the service of the King of Lydia (in modern-day Turkey), who happened upon a ring that when worn and turned in one direction made him invisible and when turned back made him visible again. Once Gyges became aware of the power of the ring, he arranged to be a messenger to the king. On arriving at the palace, he committed adultery with the queen, attacked the king with her help, killed him, and took over the kingdom.[1]

From Plato's time to the present, this story has helped to dramatically pose the question: Why should I be just or moral when I could really benefit from doing something else? In everyday life, this question may arise as:

- Why should I help people in serious need when I can enjoy using my extra income to dine in a fancy restaurant or take a Caribbean cruise?
- Why should I not cheat on my taxes when I can get away with it?
- Why should I forgo any use of resources now so that future generations can have a decent life?

These questions reflect the fundamental challenge that egoism raises to morality.

PSYCHOLOGICAL EGOISM

One form this challenge takes is Psychological Egoism. This view maintains that, despite appearances to the contrary, we actually behave self-interestedly all the time. Now this may seem to be a surprising claim. Of course, we are well aware that some people we assumed were acting primarily for the good of others later turn out to be significantly motivated by self-interest. For example, a number of years ago, many people were surprised and dismayed to learn of the very large salary being paid to William Aramony, then president of United Way of America. After Aramony was pressured to resign and later convicted of fraud, a significant drop in giving to United Way persisted for some time, with some people thinking United Way was no longer the type of public service organization they had once thought it to be.[2]

Psychological Egoism, however, does not maintain that despite appearances to the contrary, some of us are significantly motivated by self-interest. Rather, the view maintains that all of us are ultimately motivated by self-interest all the time. Moreover, if we are to credit the following story reported in the *Springfield Monitor*, Abraham Lincoln at one period of his life seems to have held the very same view.

> Mr. Lincoln once remarked to a fellow-passenger on an old-time mud-coach that all men were prompted by [self-interest] in doing good. His fellow-passenger was antagonizing this position when they were passing over a corduroy bridge that spanned a [muddy stream]. As they crossed this bridge they espied an old razorback sow on the bank making a terrible noise because her pigs had got into the [muddy stream] and were in danger of drowning. As the old coach began to climb the hill, Mr. Lincoln called out, "Driver, can't you stop just a moment?" Then Mr. Lincoln jumped out, ran back and lifted the little pigs out of the mud and water and placed them on the bank. When he returned, his companion remarked: "Now Abe, where does [self-interest] come in on this little episode?" "Why, bless your soul, Ed, that was the very essence of [self-interest]. I should have had no peace of mind all day had I gone on and left that suffering old sow worrying over those pigs. I did it to get peace of mind, don't you see?"[3]

As we can see, Lincoln held that there was no difference between his behavior and that of Ed, his fellow passenger. They both acted self-interestedly, and presumably they both wanted peace of mind. Yet Lincoln, not Ed, was motivated to prevent the piglets from drowning and secure his peace of mind in that particular way. So if we just say that both men acted self-interested, as Psychological Egoism would have us do, we lose an interesting difference between the ways the two of them were, in fact, motivated.

Consider an analogy. If we say that those who are coerced and those who are not coerced both acted freely because in some sense they both chose to act as they did, we would lose an important difference between acting under coercion and acting free from coercion. And we really don't want to lose that important difference. Similarly, if we say that those who intentionally act to promote their own interests and those who intentionally act to promote the interests of others are both acting self-interestedly because in some sense they are both satisfied with what they are doing, we would be losing an important difference between two fundamentally different kinds of motivation that people have. And we really don't want to lose that important difference either.

When Lincoln decided to save the piglets and Ed decided to remain in the coach, they both were presumably satisfied with what they did. Yet the satisfaction that each experienced does not explain why they acted differently. Rather, Lincoln's action is explained by his concern for the well-being of the piglets and their mother, while Ed's is explained by his greater concern for himself;

otherwise he could have helped Lincoln save the piglets. Lincoln too could conceivably have behaved more self-interestedly. After he got to the muddy stream, he could have reflected on how wet and muddy he was going to have to get to save the piglets and changed his mind. But he didn't.

So the interesting question here is: To what degree should people be motivated by altruism, like Lincoln, or by self-interest, like Ed, in these and other such circumstances? Because it espouses an empty, trivial thesis that is true no matter what people do, Psychological Egoism does not even try to answer this question. In contrast, Ethical Egoism does try to give an answer to just that question.

ETHICAL EGOISM

In Plato's Gyges story, as we have seen, the same sort of question is posed: Why should Gyges be moral or just when, given his magical ring, he could benefit more by acting self-interestedly? Yet we do not have to reach back to Plato, or to myth, to find examples of egoism presenting a challenge to morality.

On December 10, 2008, Bernard Madoff, the former chair of the NASDAQ Stock Market, revealed to his two sons that the investment management arm of his firm was a giant Ponzi scheme—as he put it, "one big lie." A Ponzi scheme is a fraudulent investment operation that pays returns to investors from their own money or money paid by subsequent investors rather than from profit, and so at some point the scheme has to run out of money.[4] After Madoff's sons passed this information on to the authorities, Madoff was arrested and charged with bilking his investors out of fifty billion dollar. That makes his crime the largest Ponzi scheme ever perpetrated and the largest investment fraud ever committed by a single person. By targeting charities, Madoff was also able to avoid the threat of sudden or unexpected withdrawals and thus keep his scheme going for a number of years.[5]

Surely Madoff's behavior should suffice to make him an egoist. Nevertheless, as an egoist, he made one fairly significant mistake. He didn't find a way to disappear with a good portion of his stolen funds just before his Ponzi scheme collapsed. What we need to determine, however, is, How does Ethical Egoism purport to justify the behavior of Gyges and Madoff and many other egoists like them?

To answer this question, we need to examine the two main forms that Ethical Egoism takes:

1. Individual Ethical Egoism which maintains that everyone *ought* to do what is in the overall self-interest of just one particular individual.
2. Universal Ethical Egoism which maintains that everyone *ought* to do what is in his or her own overall self-interest.

Individual Ethical Egoism

Let's begin by addressing the challenge of Individual Ethical Egoism, a view that is often not clearly distinguished from the more discussed Universal Ethical Egoism.[6] Individual Ethical Egoism maintains that everyone ought to do what is in the overall self-interest of just one particular individual. That means that all claims about what each of us ought to do are to be based on the overall interests of just one particular individual. The good of that one individual determines what everyone else ought to do.

Let's call that individual Gladys. Why do only Gladys's interests count in determining what everyone ought to do? Individual Ethical Egoism must provide us with an adequate justification for giving only Gladys's interests this status.

Consider what will *not* work to provide such a justification:

1. Any *relational characteristic*, such as Gladys being Seymour's wife, would provide justification for Gladys's special status, because other persons would have similar relational characteristics.
2. Any *characteristic shared with others*, like being a woman or a feminist, would justify favoring Gladys's interests, because it would provide the same justification for favoring the interests of all other women or feminists.
3. Any *unique characteristic*, such as Gladys knowing all of Shakespeare's writings by heart, would provide justification, because others may possess such characteristics to lesser degrees, giving them justification (although proportionally less) for favoring their own interests.
4. The mere fact of *possessing unique traits* would justify Gladys's special status, because every individual has unique traits.
5. *Claiming special status* simply because Gladys is herself and wants to further her own interests, because every other person could make the same claim.[7]

In sum, if the defender of Individual Ethical Egoism were to argue that the same or similar reasons do *not* hold for other people with the same or similar characteristics to those of Gladys, the defender must explain why they do not hold. This is because it must always be possible to understand how a characteristic serves as a reason in one case but not in another. If no explanation can be provided, and in the case of Individual Ethical Egoism none has been forthcoming, the proposed characteristic either serves as a reason in both cases or it does not serve as a reason at all.

Thus, it turns out that Individual Ethical Egoism, upon examination, is an indefensible position. It claims that everyone ought to do what serves the overall interest of just one particular individual, but it is incapable of providing any justification which could plausibly support that claim.

Universal Ethical Egoism

The Universal Ethical Egoist (let's call him Seymour) presumably starts out with the same general goal as Gladys, whose interests were to be served by Individual Ethical Egoism. Seymour too would like to show that the furthering of his own interests is the thing to do. Nevertheless, he recognizes that any reason that he could give for furthering his own interests would suggest a similar or analogous reason that others could give for furthering their interests. As a Universal Ethical Egoist, however, Seymour confronts this problem by granting that each person has similar reasons for favoring his or her own interests. In order to justify favoring his own interests, Seymour realizes that he must allow that others are similarly justified in favoring their own interests. It is this willingness to generalize that saves Universal Ethical Egoism from the fate of Individual Ethical Egoism, which refused to generalize, thereby rendering Universal Ethical Egoism a serious challenge to morality. Let us now consider three of the most important attempts to meet that challenge.

APPEALING TO PUBLICITY

Universal Ethical Egoism has been forcefully criticized by contemporary philosopher, Christine Korsgaard, among others, for failing to meet a "publicity requirement" that is satisfied by morality.[8] Those committed to morality, just like those committed to obeying the law, usually want their commitment to be publicly known so that they will be better able to resolve conflicts with others who are similarly committed. By contrast, Seymour, our Universal Ethical Egoist, is usually not going to want his commitment to Universal Ethical Egoism to be publicly known. If others know that he is an egoist, they will tend to guard themselves against being harmed by him and, as a consequence, he may not be able to benefit at their expense to the degree that he would otherwise want to do. Rather, while privately endorsing egoism, Seymour is going to publicly, yet hypocritically, profess a commitment to morality in order to secure for himself the benefit that such a public endorsement of morality provides.

Of course, privately Seymour thinks that others, like him, ought to be similarly committed to Universal Ethical Egoism, although he will never tell them so, except perhaps when their interests happen to further his own. For him to reveal his commitment to Universal Ethical Egoism on other occasions would work against his interests. There will be times when Seymour will think that others ought to interfere with him, yet because he and others are publicly committed to a morality that prohibits and attempts to punish interferences of this sort, Seymour will thereby hope to avoid such interference to himself. On other occasions, Seymour will be able to further his overall self-interest by selectively, and usually secretively, interfering with the interests of others in violation of the requirements of morality. This is exactly what Gyges was able to do in Plato's dialogue, and what Madoff was able to do in real life as well, at least for a number of years. So while Universal Ethical Egoism is not committed to the same publicity requirement that we find in morality, given its rationale for avoiding that requirement, it is difficult to see how this lack of commitment should count as grounds for rejecting the view. Clearly, keeping their commitment to egoism relatively private was essential to the success of both Gyges and Madoff.[9]

PARALLELING EGOISM AND RACISM

Recently, philosopher James Rachels offered an argument that he thinks "comes closest to an outright refutation of Ethical Egoism."[10] Rachels attempts to defeat the view by paralleling egoism with racism and then showing that they are similarly defective. He argues that just as the racist does not provide a good reason why everyone should support the racist's preferred racial group, so the egoist does not provide a good reason why everyone should support the egoist's own interests over everyone else's.

Unfortunately, although Rachels directs his argument against egoism generally, his argument works only against Individual Ethical Egoism. It does not also work against Universal Ethical Egoism, the view we are presently considering.[11] This is because only Individual Ethical Egoism wants to justify placing someone in a special category. Universal Ethical Egoism, by contrast, treats everyone the same, at least to the extent of allowing that everyone is equally justified in pursuing his or her own self-interest. So, while Rachels's argument does succeed in defeating Individual Ethical Egoism, it fails to meet the more serious challenge of Universal Ethical Egoism.

APPEALING TO CONSISTENCY

Still another attempt to meet the challenge of Universal Ethical Egoism, advanced by contemporary philosopher Kurt Baier, among others, tries to show that Universal Ethical Egoism is fundamentally inconsistent.[12] For the purpose of evaluating this critique, let's use as an example a modern Gyges, Gary Gyges by name, an otherwise normal human being who, for reasons of personal gain, has embezzled $10 million while working as an accountant at People's National Bank and is now taking steps to escape to a South Sea island where he will have the good fortune to live a pleasant life protected by the local authorities and untroubled by any qualms of conscience. Suppose that a fellow employee, Hedda Hawkeye, knows that Gary has embezzled money from the bank and is about to escape. Suppose, further, that it is in Hawkeye's overall self-interest to prevent Gyges from escaping with the embezzled money because she will be generously rewarded for doing so by being appointed vice president of the bank. Given that it is in Gary's overall self-interest to escape with the embezzled money, it now appears that we can derive a contradiction for Universal Ethical Egoism from the following:

1. Gyges ought to escape with the embezzled money.
2. Hawkeye ought to prevent Gyges from escaping with the embezzled money.
3. By preventing Gyges from escaping with the embezzled money, Hawkeye is preventing Gyges from doing what he ought to do.
4. One ought never to prevent someone from doing what he or she ought to do.
5. Thus, Hawkeye ought not to prevent Gyges from escaping with the embezzled money.

Because premise (2) and conclusion (5) are contradictory, Universal Ethical Egoism appears to be inconsistent.

The soundness of this argument depends, however, on premise (4), and Seymour, our Universal Ethical Egoist, believes there are grounds for rejecting this premise. As Seymour understands the "oughts" of Universal Ethical Egoism, he is justified in preventing others from doing what they ought to do in violation of premise (4). This is because Seymour understands them to be analogous to the "oughts" of competitive games, which do justify just this sort of behavior.

Consider, for example, how in football a defensive player might think that the opposing team's quarterback ought to pass on third down with five yards to go, while not wanting the quarterback to do so and indeed hoping to foil any such attempt the quarterback makes. Or to use contemporary philosopher Jesse Kalin's example:

> I may see how my chess opponent can put my king in check. This is how he ought to move. But believing that he ought to move his bishop and check my king does not commit me to wanting him to do that, nor to persuading him to do so. What I ought to do is sit there quietly, hoping he does not move as he ought.[13]

The point of these examples is to suggest that a Universal Ethical Egoist may, like a player in a game, judge that others ought to do what is in their overall self-interest while simultaneously attempting to prevent such actions or at least refraining from encouraging them. And this provides grounds for rejecting premise (4) from the earlier argument against Universal Ethical Egoism.

The analogy of competitive games also illustrates the sense in which a Universal Ethical Egoist claims that she herself ought to do what is in her overall self-interest. For just as a player's judgment that she ought to make a particular move is followed, other things being equal, by an attempt to perform the appropriate action (the defensive player attempting to stop the quarterback's throw), so likewise when a Universal Ethical Egoist judges that she ought to do some particular action, other things being equal, an attempt to perform the appropriate action follows (Madoff's attempt to benefit indefinitely from his Ponzi scheme).

In general, defenders of Universal Ethical Egoism stress that because we have little difficulty understanding the implications of the use of "ought" in competitive games, we should also have little difficulty understanding the analogous use of "ought" by the Universal Ethical Egoist, which in turns provides grounds for rejecting premise (4) of the argument that was supposed to show that Universal Ethical Egoism was an inconsistent view.[14]

IS THERE NO WAY TO MEET THE CHALLENGE OF UNIVERSAL ETHICAL EGOISM?

The challenge of Universal Ethical Egoism to morality has proven to be a strong one, as the failure of the previous three arguments to meet that challenge shows. In fact, due to the past failures to provide a strong defense of morality over egoism, most moral philosophers today have simply given up hope of providing an argument showing that morality is rationally preferable to egoism.[15] Rather, they seem content to show that morality is simply rationally permissible, which means that egoism is rationally permissible as well. Most contemporary moral philosophers do not think anything more can be established.

While this consensus among moral philosophers today is quite strong, a few philosophers express hope that we can do better and actually provide arguments showing that morality is rationally required and not just simply rationally permissible.[16] Most moral philosophers today would certainly like to have a good argument of this sort. So given the importance of the question of whether morality can be shown to be rationally required, let us consider just one more attempt to meet the challenge of Universal Ethical Egoism and show that morality is rationally preferable to it.

From Rationality to Morality

Let us begin by imagining that each of us is capable of entertaining and acting upon both self-interested and moral reasons and that the question we are seeking to answer is what sort of reasons for action it would be rational for us to accept.[17] This question is not about what sort of reasons we should publicly affirm, since people will sometimes publicly affirm reasons that are quite different from those they are prepared to act upon. Rather, this question focuses on what reasons it would be rational for us to accept at the deepest level—in our heart of hearts—when we are speaking truthfully to ourselves.

Granted, some people are incapable of acting upon moral reasons. For such people, there is no question about their being required to act morally or altruistically. Yet the interesting philosophical question is not about them but about people, like ourselves, who are capable of acting morally as well as self-interestedly and are seeking a rational justification for following a particular course of action.

In trying to determine how we should act, let us assume that we would like to be able to construct a *good* argument favoring morality over egoism. Given that good arguments are nonquestion-begging, they do not assume what they are trying to prove.

In a film by Sacha Guitry, three thieves are arguing over the division of some very valuable pearls. One of the thieves gives two to the thief on his right, then two to the thief on his left. "I," he says, "will keep three." "How come you get to keep three?" one of the other two thieves asks. "Because I am the leader," he replies. "Oh. But how come you are the leader?" asks the other thief. "Because I have more pearls," he replies. In the film, this question-begging argument that assumes just what it purports to prove surprisingly satisfies the other two thieves because they do not further question how the pearls have been distributed. However, let's assume that we would like to do better by constructing a good argument for morality that does not similarly beg the question.[18]

The question at issue here is what reasons each of us should take as supreme, and this question would be begged against Universal Ethical Egoism (hereafter simply egoism) if we proposed to answer it simply by assuming from the start that moral reasons are the reasons that each of us should take as supreme. But the question would be begged against morality as well if we proposed to answer the question simply by assuming from the start that self-interested reasons are the reasons that each of us should take as supreme. This means, of course, that we cannot answer the question of what reasons we should take as supreme simply by assuming the general principle of egoism: *Each person ought to do what best serves his or her overall self-interest.*

We can no more argue for egoism simply by denying the relevance of moral reasons to rational choice than we can argue for altruism simply by denying the relevance of self-interested reasons to rational choice and assuming the general principle of altruism: *Each person ought to do what best serves the overall interest of others.*[19]

This means that we can no more argue for egoism simply by denying the relevance of moral reasons to rational choice than we can argue for altruism simply by denying the relevance of self-interested reasons to rational choice. Consequently, we have no other alternative but to grant the *prima facie* relevance of both self-interested and altruistic reasons to rational choice and then try to determine which reasons we would be rationally required to act upon, all things considered. (Notice that in order not to beg the question, it is necessary to back off from both the general principle of egoism and from the general principle of altruism. From this standpoint, it is still an open question, whether egoism or altruism will be rationally preferable.)

This leaves us to consider two kinds of cases: cases in which there is a conflict between the relevant self-interested and moral or altruistic reasons and cases in which there is no such conflict.

It seems obvious that where there is no conflict and both reasons are conclusive reasons of their kind, both reasons should be acted upon. In such contexts, we should do what is favored both by morality or altruism and by self-interest.

Consider the following example. Suppose you accepted a job marketing a baby formula in a developing country where the formula was improperly used leading to increased infant mortality.[20] Imagine that you could just as well have accepted an equally attractive and rewarding job, marketing a similar formula in a developed country where the misuse does not occur so that a rational weighing of the relevant self-interested reasons alone would not have favored your acceptance of one of these jobs over the other.[21] At the same time, there were obviously moral reasons that condemned your acceptance of the first job—reasons that you presumably are or were able to acquire. Moreover, by assumption in this case, the moral reasons do not clash with the relevant self-interested reasons; they simply made a recommendation where the relevant self-interested reasons were silent. Consequently, a rational weighing of all the relevant reasons in this case could not but favor acting in accord with both the relevant self-interested and moral reasons.

Now when we rationally assess the relevant reasons in conflict cases, it is best to cast the conflict not as a conflict between self-interested reasons and moral reasons but instead as a conflict between self-interested reasons and altruistic reasons.[22] Viewed in this way, three solutions are possible:

- Self-interested reasons always have priority over conflicting altruistic reasons.
- Altruistic reasons always have priority over conflicting self-interested reasons.
- Some kind of compromise is rationally required. In this compromise, sometimes self-interested reasons would have priority over altruistic reasons, and sometimes altruistic reasons would have priority over self-interested reasons.

Once the conflict is described in this manner, the third solution can be seen to be the one that is rationally required. This is because the first and second solutions give exclusive priority to one class of relevant reasons over the other, and only a question-begging justification can be given for such an exclusive priority. Only by employing the third solution—sometimes giving priority to self-interested reasons, sometimes giving priority to altruistic reasons—can we avoid a question-begging resolution.

For example, suppose that you are in the waste disposal business and you have decided to dispose of toxic wastes in a manner that is cost-efficient for you but predictably causes significant harm to future generations. Imagine that there are alternative methods available for disposing of the waste that are only slightly less cost-efficient and will not cause any significant harm to future generations.[23] In this case, you would weigh your self-interested reasons favoring the most cost-efficient disposal of the toxic wastes against the relevant altruistic reasons favoring the avoidance of significant harm to future generations. If we suppose that the projected loss of benefit to yourself was ever so slight and the projected harm to future generations was ever so great, then a nonarbitrary compromise between the relevant self-interested and altruistic reasons would have to favor the altruistic reasons. Hence, as judged by a nonquestion-begging standard of rationality, your method of waste disposal was contrary to the relevant reasons.

Notice also that this standard of rationality will not support just any compromise between the relevant self-interested and altruistic reasons. The compromise must be a nonarbitrary one, for otherwise it would beg the question with respect to the opposing egoistic or altruistic perspective.[24] Such a compromise would have to respect the rankings of self-interested and altruistic reasons imposed by the egoistic and altruistic perspectives, respectively. Accordingly, any nonarbitrary compromise among such reasons in seeking not to beg the question against either egoism or altruism will have to give priority to those reasons that rank highest in each category. Failure to give priority to the highest-ranking altruistic or self-interested reasons would, other things being equal, be contrary to reason.

Lifeboat Cases

Of course, there will be cases in which the only way to avoid being required to do what is contrary to your highest-ranking reasons is by requiring someone else to do what is contrary to his or her highest-ranking reasons. Some of these cases will be so-called lifeboat cases, as when two individuals are stranded in a lifeboat that has only enough resources for one to survive. Although such cases are surely difficult to resolve (maybe only a chance mechanism, like flipping a coin, can offer a reasonable resolution), they surely do not reflect the typical conflict between the relevant self-interested and altruistic reasons that we are or were able to acquire. Typically, one or the other of the conflicting reasons will rank significantly higher on its respective scale, thus permitting a clear resolution.

MORALITY AS COMPROMISE

We can see how morality can be viewed as a nonarbitrary compromise between self-interested and altruistic reasons. First, a certain amount of self-regard is morally required or at least morally acceptable. Where this is the case, high-ranking self-interested reasons have priority over low-ranking altruistic reasons. Second, morality obviously places limits on the extent to which people should pursue their own self-interest. Where this is the case, high-ranking altruistic reasons have priority over low-ranking self-interested reasons. In this way, morality can be seen to be a nonarbitrary compromise between self-interested and altruistic reasons, and the "moral reasons" that constitute that compromise can be seen as having an absolute priority over the self-interested or altruistic reasons that conflict with them.[25]

Yet does Morality as Compromise provide an answer to the egoism as practiced by Gyges in myth and by Madoff in reality? Well, it does provide a good, that is, a nonquestion-begging argument favoring morality over egoism and in this way justifies morality over egoism. Of course, this may not have the hoped-for effect on real-life egoists. They may not care whether there is a good argument or justification for what they are doing or proposing to do. To deal with them, we may have to resort to avoidance or coercion. If we do need to resort to coercion, however, Morality as Compromise can also provide us with a good argument for doing so. What more then could we expect it to do to enable us to face the challenge of egoism?

Of course, exactly how Morality as Compromise is to be implemented in practice needs to be determined. So far developed, it is open to a number of different interpretations. A utilitarian approach would seemingly favor one sort of interpretation of the compromise, a Kantian approach another, and an Aristotelian approach yet another, as we will see in subsequent chapters. So Morality as Compromise is anything but a decision procedure for solving practical moral problems. Nevertheless, however this debate between alternative interpretations is resolved, it is clear that some sort of a compromise view or moral solution is rationally preferable to either egoism or altruism when judged from a nonquestion-begging standpoint. Surely, that should suffice to answer the challenge of egoism.

Conclusion

In this chapter, we have seen that the challenge of Psychological Egoism to ethics is based on the empty thesis that people are in some sense satisfied with whatever they do, thus ignoring the different ways that self-interested and altruistic reasons produce that satisfaction. Not faring much better, the challenge of Individual Ethical Egoism showed itself to be incapable of providing any justification that could plausibly support the view. By contrast, Universal Ethical Egoism showed itself a formidable challenge to ethics, easily turning aside objections appealing to the publicity of reasons, to parallels between egoism and racism, and to consistency. As we saw, this challenge could only effectively be met by a non-question-begging argument that favored morality over both egoism and altruism.

MySearchLab Connections

Watch. Listen. Explore. Read. MySearchLab is designed just for you. Each chapter features a customized study plan to help you learn key concepts and terms. Dynamic visual activities, videos, and readings found in the multimedia library will enhance your learning experience.

Here are a few questions and activities to help you understand this chapter:

1. What are some other arguments against Psychological Egoism (pp. 38–39)?

   Read "Psychological Egoism," Multimedia Library, Web Resources, Internet Encyclopedia of Philosophy.

2. What are some other arguments against Ethical Egoism (p. 39ff)?

   Read "Egoism," Multimedia Library, Web Resources, Stanford Encyclopedia of Philosophy.

Each chapter features a customized study plan to help you learn and review key concepts and terms.

Notes

1. Plato, *The Republic*, trans. G. M. A . Grube (Indianapolis: Hackett, 1974), Book II.
2. William P. Barrett, "United Way's New Way," *Forbes*, January 16, 2006, http://www.forbes.com/2006/01/13/united-way-philanthropy-cz_wb_0117unitedway.html.
3. As quoted in *Outlook 56 (1897)*: 1059. The original story used "selfishness" in each place that I have inserted "self-interest." But I think my usage captures the intent of the original story better than its own usage. This is because "selfishness" conveys the sense of "an excessive concern for oneself." But the original story did not intend to convey that meaning at all by its use of the term. By its use of "selfishness," the story just meant to convey "self-interest."

4. Ponzi schemes are named after Charles Ponzi who became notorious for using the technique in the early twentieth century.

5. David Voreacos and David Glovin, "Madoff Confessed $50 Billion Fraud Before FBI Arrest," *Bloomberg News*, December 13, 2008, http://www.bloomberg.com/apps/news?pid=newsarchive&sid=atUk.QnXAvZY.

6. James Rachels, as we shall see, confounds these two forms of egoism, taking an argument that works against Individual Ethical Egoism to also work against Universal Ethical Egoism when it doesn't. See the discussion later in this text.

7. For further argument on this point, see Marcus Singer, *Generalization in Ethics* (New York: Alfred A. Knopf, 1961), Chapter 2; Alan Gewirth, "The Non-Trivializability of Universalizability," *Australasian Journal of Philosophy* (1969), 123–131.

8. Christine Korsgaard, "The Sources of Normativity," *The Tanner Lectures on Human Values* (Salt Lake City: University of Utah Press, 1992), 20–112. Although Korsgaard puts her publicity objection to egoism somewhat differently than I have here—she compares egoism to a private language—the egoist's response to both forms of the objection is the same.

9. It should be clear that both Gyges and Madoff are committed to Universal Ethical Egoism, and not to Individual Ethical Egoism, because their behavior nowhere suggests that they are the only ones who should be acting egoistically.

10. James Rachels and Stuart Rachels, *The Elements of Moral Philosophy,* 7th ed. (New York: McGraw-Hill, 2012), 79–81.

11. Rachels fails to distinguish between these two forms of egoism, blurring them together. This explains why he doesn't see that his argument against the one form of egoism does not work against the other. But he is not alone in failing to distinguish these two forms of egoism. See also Robert Holmes, *Basic Moral Philosophy,* 4th ed. (Belmont, CA: Wadsworth Publishing Co., 2006), Chapter 5; Gordon Graham, *Living the Good Life: An Introduction to Moral Philosophy* (New York: Paragon, 1990), Chapter 1.

12. Kurt Baier, *The Moral Point of View* (Ithaca: Cornell University Press, 1958), 188–191.

13. Jesse Kalin, "In Defense of Egoism," in *Morality and Rational Self-Interest*, ed. David Gauthier (Englewood Cliffs, NJ: Prentice Hall, 1970), 73–74.

14. To claim, however, that the "oughts" in competitive games are analogous to the "oughts" of Universal Ethical Egoism does not mean there are no differences between them. Most importantly, competitive games are governed by moral constraints such that when everyone plays the game properly, there are acceptable moral limits as to what one can do. For example, in football, one cannot poison the opposing quarterback in order to win the game. By contrast, when everyone holds self-interested reasons to be supreme, the only limit to what one can do is the point beyond which one ceases to benefit. But this important difference between the "oughts" of Universal Ethical Egoism and the "oughts" found in publicly recognized activities like competitive games does not defeat the appropriateness of the analogy. That the "oughts" found in publicly recognized activities are always limited by various moral constraints (what else would get publicly recognized?) does not preclude their being a suggestive model for the unlimited action-guiding character of the "oughts" of Universal Ethical Egoism.

15. John Rawls is typical here, as is Thomas Nagel. See John Rawls, *A Theory of Justice* (Cambridge: Harvard University Press, 1971), 136; Thomas Nagel, *The View from Nowhere* (New York: Oxford University Press), 200ff.

16. See, for example, Christine Korsgaard, *The Sources of Normativity*, (Cambridge: Cambridge University Press, 1996).

17. "Ought" presupposes "can" here. So unless people have the capacity to entertain and follow both self-interested and moral reasons for acting, it does not make any sense asking whether they ought or ought not to do so. Moreover, moral reasons here are understood to necessarily include (some) altruistic reasons but not necessarily to exclude (all) self-interested reasons. So the question of whether it would be rational for us to follow self-interested reasons rather than moral reasons should be understood as the question of whether it would be rational for us to follow self-interested reasons exclusively rather than an appropriate set of self-interested reasons and altruistic reasons that can be taken to constitute the class of moral reasons.

18. For a discussion of other features of good arguments that fortunately are not at issue with regard to providing a justification of morality over egoism, see Merrie Bergmann, James Moor, and Jack Nelson, *The Logic Book* (New York: McGraw-Hill, 2008).

19. The altruist is here understood to be the mirror image of the egoist. Whereas the egoist thinks that the interests of others count for them but not for herself except instrumentally, the altruist thinks that her own interests count for others, but not for herself except instrumentally.

20. For a discussion of the causal links involved here, see *Marketing and Promotion of Infant Formula in Developing Countries: Hearings Before the Subcommittee on International Economic Policy and Trade of the Committee on Foreign Affairs, House of Representatives, Ninety-Sixth Congress, Second Session, January 30 and February 11, 1980* (Washington, DC: GPO, 1980). See also Maggie McComas et al., *The Dilemma of Third World Nutrition,* Nestle S. A. (1983).

21. Assume that both jobs have the same beneficial effects on the interests of others.

22. This is because, as we shall see, morality itself already represents a compromise between egoism and altruism. So to ask that moral reasons be weighed against self-interested reasons is, in effect, to count self-interested reasons twice—once in the compromise between egoism and altruism and then again when moral reasons are weighed against self-interested reasons. But to count self-interested reasons twice is clearly to show a rationally inappropriate bias in favor of such reasons.

23. Assume that all these methods of waste disposal have roughly the same amount of beneficial effects on the interests of others.

24. Notice that by "egoistic perspective" here I mean the view that grants the prima facie relevance of both egoistic and altruistic reasons to rational choice and then tries to argue for the superiority of egoistic reasons. Similarly by "altruistic perspective" I mean the view that grants the prima facie relevance of both egoistic and altruistic reasons to rational choice and then tries to argue for the superiority of altruistic reasons.

25. For further discussion, see James P. Sterba, "Completing the Kantian Project: From Rationality to Equality," Presidential Address to the APA, *Proceedings and Addresses of the American Philosophical Association 82,* no. 2 (November 2008).

CHAPTER **4**

Utilitarian Ethics

The first Sunday after 9/11, then Vice President Dick Cheney, appearing on *Meet the Press*, gave a memorable statement of how the Bush administration planned to deal with the threat posed by the terrorist attack on the World Trade Center and the Pentagon:

> We'll have to work sort of the dark side, if you will. We've got to spend time in the shadows in the intelligence world. A lot of what needs to be done here will have to be done quietly, without any discussion, using sources and methods that are available to our intelligences agencies—if we are to be successful. That's the world these folks operate in.... [S]o it's going to be vital for us to use any means at our disposal basically, to achieve our objectives.[1]

We now know a lot more of what Cheney meant by this shift in U.S. policy following 9/11. It involved releasing our military forces, the CIA in particular, from the constraints of the Geneva Conventions. Under the Geneva Conventions, detainees had to be treated humanely.[2] They could not be punished for refusing to cooperate with interrogators and they had to be given access to the Red Cross. "No physical or mental torture or any other form of coercion may be inflicted on prisoners of war to secure from them information of any kind whatsoever," the Conventions stated. In addition, every captive was entitled to a hearing before a competent tribunal in order to determine his or her status. Even during the Vietnam War, when the North Vietnamese refused to regard U.S. pilots, like John McCain, as legitimately covered by the Geneva Conventions, calling them "pirates" in an illegal war, thus, in the minds of the North Vietnamese, permitting their use of torture to obtain information, the United States continued to respect the Conventions as applying to the North Vietnamese and the Vietcong.

In addition, although the UN Convention Against Torture prohibited any signee from "expelling, extraditing or otherwise effecting the involuntary removal of any person to a country where there are substantial grounds for believing the person would be in danger of being subject to torture," the Bush administration following 9/11, regularly availed themselves of such renditions to states like Egypt, Monaco, Syria, Jordan, Uzbekistan, and Afghanistan, all of which were known, at the time, to torture and had long been cited for human rights violations by the U.S. State Department. Syria, for example, was known for "administering electric shocks, pulling out finger nails, forcing objects up the rectum and hyper-extending the spine" to the point of "fracture." In Egypt, detainees "were stripped and blindfolded, suspended from a ceiling or door frame with feet just touching the floor; beaten with fists, whips, metal rods, or other objects; subjected to electric shocks, and doused with cold water [and] sexually assaulted."

INTRODUCING UTILITARIAN ETHICS

One ethical theory that may, however, justify such acts of torture is utilitarianism. This theory was first proposed by Mo Tzu in China around 450 BC, and for a time it presented a challenge to the dominant Confucianism. In the West, however, the theory traces its origins to Francis Hutchinson (1723–1790), David Hume (1711–1776), and its most canonical formulations to Jeremy Bentham (1748–1832) and John Stuart Mill (1806–1873). In 1806, a meeting between Bentham and James Mill (John Stuart Mill's father) led to the formation of a group called the Philosophical Radicals, who pressed for political and social reforms. John Stuart Mill, a child prodigy, studied Greek at 3, Latin at 8, wrote a history of Roman law at 10, and at 15 undertook a study of Bentham's writings. Subsequently, guided by his father, he became intensely involved in the work of the Philosophical Radicals.

For Bentham, there was one ultimate principle of morality, namely, the Principle of Utility, which requires us to always choose whatever action or social policy would have the best consequences for everyone concerned. As Bentham put it in his book, *The Principles of Morals and Legislation*:

> By the Principle of Utility is meant that principle which approves or disapproves of every action whatsoever, according to the tendency which it appears to have to augment or diminish the happiness of the party whose interest is in question...

But who is "the party whose interest is in question" for utilitarians? Mill made it perfectly clear that it was everyone who could be affected by the action in question:

> [T]he happiness which forms the utilitarian standard of what is right in conduct, is not the agent's own happiness, but that of all concerned. As between his own happiness and that of others, utilitarianism requires him to be strictly impartial as a disinterested and benevolent spectator.

In his own day, Bentham appealed to this utilitarian standard to support the separation of church and state, freedom of expression, the end of slavery, free trade, the decriminalization of homosexuality, and the elimination of the death penalty. Mill used it to support universal male suffrage, proportional representation, labor unions, and farm cooperatives. In 1869, Mill also published *The Subjection of Women* in which he argued for gender equality on utilitarian grounds.

Bentham understood happiness to be pleasure and he understood pleasures not to differ in quality. Thus, he famously remarked that pushpin (a children's game) is as good as poetry, in that, as he saw it, they both provided the same kind of pleasure.[3] While Mill too equated happiness with pleasure, he disagreed with Bentham in holding that pleasures can vary in quality. Thus, for Mill, playing pushpin and reading Shakespearean sonnets provided qualitatively different kinds of pleasure. Mill also held that qualitatively higher pleasures were those that would be preferred by competent judges who had experienced the alternatives. Using this standard, Mill also famously claimed that "it is better to be a human being dissatisfied than a pig satisfied; better to be Socrates dissatisfied than a fool satisfied." Obviously no competent human judge, as far as we know, has become a real pig and then returned to human form to tell us what that experience was like. Accordingly, what Mill must have been doing here is simply berating fellow humans, who, unlike real pigs, fail to take advantage of the full range of pleasures available to them, given their nature.

Still, critics have pointed out that other things contribute to our good, and so to our happiness, that are not pleasures that we personally experience. For example, when someone is prevented from slandering us, our good is served, even if we never hear about the slander or experience its effects. We also think it is important to maintain certain relationships with others, particularly friendships, at least in part, irrespective of any pleasures we or anyone else happen to derive from them. Accordingly, contemporary utilitarians have come to understand happiness more broadly than Bentham and Mill to include anything that contributes to our good or to the good of others.

AN IMPLICATION OF UTILITARIAN ETHICS: SACRIFICING THE FEW FOR THE MANY

Yet whether a person's happiness is understood broadly or narrowly, utilitarians have always allowed that the happiness or good of a few can be sacrificed if it results in greater happiness or good for many others, and so greater happiness or good overall. Drawing on David Hume, contemporary defenders of utilitarian ethics sometimes claim that what utilitarianism requires is what an ideally sympathetic agent, with knowledge of everyone's interests, would approve of. Accordingly, it would be permissible according to utilitarianism to tax the rich to secure a decent minimum for the poor, provided that the benefit to the poor is greater than any consequent loss to the rich.

So could utilitarianism be similarly used to justify the practice of torturing detainees as a way of achieving a greater good overall? One could question whether the actions that the Bush administration authorized against detainees did, in fact, constitute torture. What was authorized did include such practices as waterboarding, or suffocation by drowning, which had long been thought to be torture under the Geneva Conventions and had been prosecuted as such after World War II at the Tokyo Trials and by the United States as recently as 1983.

Yet Bush administration lawyers redefined torture so that waterboarding in itself did not constitute torture. According to Jay Bybee, at the time the head of the Office of Legal Counsel in the U.S. Department of Justice, "physical pain amounting to torture must be equivalent in intensity to the pain accompanying serious physical injury, such as organ failure, impairment of bodily function or even death," and "for purely mental pain or suffering to amount to torture, it must result in significant psychological harm of significant duration, e.g., lasting months or even years."[4] So maybe what was done to detainees by the CIA and the U.S. military did not constitute torture so defined.

But let's not alter or go against long-standing internationally recognized definitions of torture here. Let's allow that waterboarding, or something still worse, is torture and then ask whether it could be justified by the good outcome that would result from subjecting detainees to such treatment.[5] Presumably the justification for the United States to be engaged in torture is to extract information from detainees that could be used to prevent further harm to the United States or its citizens, or for some other good purpose.[6] In other words, if torture is justified, it would have to be a means of producing the best consequences overall. Of course, detainees would suffer from being tortured, but the compensating benefit to others would have to justify that suffering. That is how a utilitarian justification might be given for the use of torture in Guantanamo, Abu Ghraib, or in any of the black site retention centers to which the CIA sent detainees for interrogation.

OSAMA BIN LADEN AND TERRORISM

Yet if we could justify the torture of detainees on the basis of the overall good consequences that result, why could not acts of terrorism be similarly justified on the same consequential basis?

Consider that act of terrorism Americans know best—9/11. That act began on a clear, early autumn morning in New York. At 8:45 a.m., a hijacked American Airlines passenger plane piloted by Muhamed Atta slammed into the north tower of New York City's World Trade Center. Within twenty minutes, a second hijacked United Airlines plane piloted by Marwan al-Shehhi struck the south tower. At 9:45 a.m., another hijacked plane crashed into the western façade of the Pentagon, and less than a half hour later, a fourth hijacked plane plummeted to the earth in a wooded field outside Somerset, Pennsylvania. At 9:50 a.m., the south tower of the World Trade Center began to collapse, each floor pancaking onto the one below. Forty minutes later, the north tower seemed to implode. The collapse of the Twin Towers sent dust and smoke billowing through the streets of Lower Manhattan as thousands of terrified New Yorkers ran for cover. Initial estimates put the number of dead from this terrorist attack at over 5,000, but later the death toll was determined to be 2,974.

Suppose someone were to claim that 9/11 is justified because of its consequences. If we were utilitarians, we couldn't just reject that possibility without an examination of the consequences. We would have to determine what
benefits bin Laden and al-Qaeda derived from 9/11, and we would have to
look at other consequences too. If we were utilitarians, we couldn't just dismiss
such claims out of hand.

So what have been the consequences of 9/11? First, there was the U.S.
military intervention in Afghanistan. Surely, bin Laden expected that intervention. Nevertheless, he probably thought U.S. forces would get bogged down
in a ground war in Afghanistan just the way the Russians had in the 1980s. Although U.S. forces did initially avoid being bogged down, a recent resurgence
of al-Qaeda and Taliban forces in Afghanistan that spread to Pakistan has left
in doubt whether, and to what degree, bin Laden, now killed by U.S. special
forces near the capital of Pakistan, and al-Qaeda might still have benefited from
this intervention.

However, what is not in doubt is that the main benefit of 9/11 for bin
Laden came about in a way that he most assuredly did not directly expect—
through the U.S. invasion and occupation of Iraq. The cost of that military
intervention for the United States to date has been more than 4,000 dead, over
30,000 wounded, and a currently estimated financial cost of four trillion dol-
lars.[7] The financial cost of the war alone imposes a significant burden on the
United States that surely limits its military options in the near future. The United
States cannot now fight four-trillion-dollar wars against al-Qaeda–inspired
insurrections elsewhere, say in Egypt or Saudi Arabia. This limitation on what
the United States can now do, resulting from its invasion and occupation of Iraq,
therefore, converts into a benefit for bin Laden. This is because bin Laden's goal
was to limit and diminish U.S. power, particularly in the Middle East.

So does this mean that 9/11 was justified on utilitarian grounds because of the benefits that bin Laden and al-Qaeda derived from it? Does
this also mean that acts of torture as practiced by the CIA and the U.S.
military were justified on utilitarian grounds because of the benefits that
we in the United States derive from them? Not necessarily. Among other
things, this is because utilitarianism requires that all, not just some, of the
consequences of an action be taken into account in assessing its justification. So we need to consider the harms caused by these actions as well as
their benefits.

Even so, we do seem to be able to find cases where the irreparable
harm inflicted on some appears to be outweighed by the overall benefit to
others. Surely, Cheney thought that the acts of torture inflicted on detainees
by the CIA and the U.S. military are justified by their good consequences for
others. And just as surely, Osama bin Laden and his followers thought that
the deaths and destruction of 9/11 are justified by their good consequences,
particularly in the Middle East. Nevertheless, according to utilitarian ethics,
whether such acts of torture or terror are justified depends on whether the
significant harms inflicted on some are, in fact, outweighed by greater benefits to others.

HYPOTHETICAL EXAMPLES

To better illustrate the possibility of justifying inflicting significant harms on some for the sake of greater benefit to others, philosophers have frequently proposed hypothetical examples where, unlike in real-life examples, all the relevant facts that characterize the examples can be definitively specified by just stipulating them to be thus and so.

Consider the following example. A talented transplant surgeon happens to have five patients; two need lung transplants and the other three need heart, liver, and kidney transplants, respectively. Each of them will die shortly without the required transplant. Unfortunately, there are no organs from legitimate sources available to perform any of these transplant operations. However, a healthy young male, who just happens to be passing through, comes to see the doctor for a routine checkup. In the course of the checkup, with speedy lab work, the doctor discovers that the young man's organs are compatible with all five of her dying patients. Suppose further that the young male has no surviving relatives or close friends so that if he were to disappear, no one would suspect anything untoward has happened. So would there not be good utilitarian grounds for carving up the young male and transplanting his organs to save the five terminal patients?

Or consider the following example.[8] A large person, who is leading a party of spelunkers, gets himself stuck in the mouth of a cave in which flood waters are rising. The trapped party of spelunkers just happens to have a stick of dynamite with which they can blast the large person out of the mouth of the cave. Imagine the large person's head is inside the cave, so either the spelunkers use the dynamite to blast him out of the mouth of the cave or they all drown, the large person with them. In this example, it is difficult to deny the moral permissibility of dynamiting the large person out of the mouth of the cave. After all, if that were not done, the whole party of spelunkers would die, the large person with them. So the sacrifice imposed on the large person in this example would not be that great.

Now suppose the large person's head is outside rather than inside the cave. Under those circumstances, the large person would not die when the other spelunkers drown. Presumably after slimming down a bit, he would eventually just squeeze his way out of the mouth of the cave. In this example, could the party of spelunkers trapped in the cave still legitimately use the stick of dynamite they have to save themselves rather than the large person?

This version of the spelunker example is very similar to the other examples we have been considering, since they all involve imposing irreparable suffering or death on some in order to provide a greater benefit to others. Former Vice President Cheney defends torturing detainees in order to provide greater benefits to others. Osama bin Laden surely believed that the death and destruction of 9/11 was justified because of the benefits they produced, particularly in the Middle East. Similarly, our hypothetical surgeon was proposing to save the lives of five of her terminally ill patients by carving up one perfectly healthy young man. So does utilitarianism approve of these actions? If it does, is that reason enough for us to think that utilitarianism is a morally objectionable view? To determine this, we need to lay out more clearly exactly what is supposed to be objectionable about utilitarianism.

AN OBJECTION TO UTILITARIAN ETHICS: NEVER DO EVIL

Now it is sometimes thought that what is morally objectionable about utilitarianism is not just that it would make such actions as we have been considering legitimate, but that, more generally, it would legitimize imposing any harm on some (innocent individuals) in order to secure greater benefit for others. Some would invoke the principle "Never do evil that good may come of it" in this context as expressing the appropriate anti-utilitarian sentiment. Yet this cannot be what, if anything, is morally objectionable about utilitarianism. This is because any defensible moral theory, at least in some circumstances, will justify imposing at least some harm on innocent individuals when it is trivial or reparable to secure greater benefit for others.

Suppose, for example, that the only way a doctor can get out of a crowded subway to attend to an emergency is by stepping on a few people's toes. Surely, the harm that the doctor inflicts on those innocent individuals whose toes he steps upon would be justified in any defensible moral theory by the greater benefit the doctor would be able to accomplish in the emergency situation. In this example, the harm inflicted for the sake of the greater benefit is trivial. In other examples, however, the harm inflicted is not trivial, but it is still reparable, as when one might lie to a temporarily depressed friend to keep her from committing suicide—an act for which she will be profusely grateful later. So here too any defensible moral theory would hold that the harm inflicted on an innocent person in this example is justified by the greater benefit that results.

Yet what about examples where the harm inflicted is neither trivial nor reparable? All of our earlier examples were of this sort: Cheney's use of torture, bin Laden's use of terror, the surgeon's harvesting the healthy man's organs, and the spelunkers' use of the large person. In such examples, however, similar to the last, we could imagine significant benefits accruing to a large number of people (e.g., one hundred, one thousand, one million, whatever number you want) that would be lost unless one particular (innocent) individual were seriously harmed or killed. Surely, *at some point*, any defensible moral theory will justify such sacrifices. So what is morally wrong with utilitarianism, if anything, cannot be that it justifies doing harm to innocents in order to secure a greater benefit for others. As we just noted, any defensible moral theory will have to do that on some occasions. Rather, what must be morally wrong with utilitarianism, if it is a truly objectionable moral theory, must be that it permits or requires harms of this sort when the trade-offs cannot be justified.

REFINING AND ANSWERING THE OBJECTION: NECESSARY HARM AND INDEPENDENT REASONS

So when are such trade-offs not justified? Surely, they are not justified when the same benefits could be secured in some other feasible way that would result in considerably less harm. To be morally justified the harm inflicted must be a necessary means for achieving the good results.

Of course, in a hypothetically specified example like the large person stuck in the mouth of the cave, we can just stipulate that the good results could not have been gotten in any other way and so force the conclusion that dynamiting the large person out of the mouth of the cave is the only way of securing the desired result. In real-life examples, however, this condition is often not met.

Consider our earlier examples. Cheney claimed that the torture of detainees was necessary to obtain important information, but the FBI who questioned some of the same detainees claimed that the really important information that had been gotten from these detainees had been elicited beforehand, without the use of torture.[9] So it is far from clear that torture was a necessary means for achieving the good results that Cheney sought, as would be required if torture were to be justified by utilitarianism. Similarly, in the example of Osama bin Laden, it appears that he could have achieved the same good results he sought—lessening of U.S. power in the Middle East—without using terror, that is, without directly attacking nonmilitary targets. For example, suppose that instead of targeting the World Trade Center, bin Laden had targeted several of the five U.S. military academies and the Pentagon. Surely the Bush administration would most likely have responded pretty much as it did, leading to the same costly war in Iraq that has lessened the ability of the United States to project its power in the Middle East. Nor were the deaths of the noncombatants onboard the hijacked planes necessary to achieve bin Laden's political goal. If cargo planes had been hijacked and their pilots parachuted to safety, bin Laden's political goals might even have been better achieved. So here too, it is far from clear that bin Laden's acts of terror on 9/11 were a necessary means for achieving the good results he wanted, as would be required if the terror of 9/11 were to be justified by utilitarianism.

As we noted in the crises faced by the surgeon and the trapped group of spelunkers, hypothetical examples can be stipulatively specified so that their good consequences can be realized only by the proposed means. Real-life contexts are rarely so simple. For example, we can easily think of human organ transplant schemes that don't require the sacrifice of innocent people's lives. Most, if not all, of our human organ transplant needs could be met if there were laws that required that after people died, their organs, or maybe just the organs of those who were accident victims, are made available for possible transplants through some equitable distribution system. So again here, the proposed harmful means would not be necessary, at least in real life, for achieving the desired goals.

In the final analysis, we cannot easily justify imposing irreparable harm on some to achieve overall benefit to others by appealing to a utilitarian moral theory when the harms and benefits have not been appropriately specified. This is also particularly true in real-life circumstances, where there almost always seems to be alternative ways of achieving the desired consequences that avoid the irreparable harm—alternatives that would be favored by utilitarianism. What this shows is that utilitarianism is clearly far less objectionable than some have claimed. When all the alternatives are taken into account, especially in real-life examples, it is not very likely that the view will, in fact, justify imposing irreparable harm on some innocent individuals in order to secure greater benefit for others.

Still, we would like to have stronger grounds for saying that utilitarianism would not justify such impositions other than by simply claiming that just *as a matter of fact* it would not do so. Instead, we would like to be able to have an independent reason for claiming that such impositions are not justified. Is there such a reason?

To better answer this question, let us first consider another defense of utilitarianism that also attempts to defend the view against the possibility of imposing irreparable harm on innocent individuals to secure greater benefit for others by distinguishing between two forms of utilitarianism: act utilitarianism and rule utilitarianism.

A FURTHER DEFENSE: ACT UTILITARIANISM AND RULE UTILITARIANISM

Act utilitarianism holds that an act is right if and only if it would maximize the good overall more than any other alternative act. Rule utilitarianism holds that an act is right if and only if that act is required by a rule that would maximize the good overall more than any other alternative rule, if consistently followed.

Now this defense of utilitarianism maintains that while act utilitarianism sometimes does justify imposing irreparable harm on innocent individuals in order to secure greater benefit for others, rule utilitarianism never does. Thus, rule utilitarianism is thought to uphold just the kind of constraint on the imposition of harm on innocents that is desired.

Consider how this defense is supposed to work for our example of the surgeon harvesting a healthy man's organs. In that hypothetical example, act utilitarianism is taken to require the harvesting of the healthy man's organs to save five terminally ill patients, while rule utilitarianism is taken to prohibit that harvesting because the rule that is supposed to maximize the good overall, if consistently followed, is "Don't harvest healthy people's organs."

Now it does look, like in the stipulated conditions, that act utilitarianism would require the harvesting, although, as we noted before, that would not likely obtain in real-life conditions. Yet would rule utilitarianism prohibit that action in the stipulated conditions? Surely it would if the relevant rule were "Don't harvest healthy people's organs," because then any act of harvesting people's organs would be prohibited. Yet how do we know that this particular rule rather than any alternative rule, if consistently followed, would maximize the good overall? Of course, this particular rule, if consistently followed, would better maximize the good overall than a rule that was generally permissive about the harvesting of healthy people's organs.

But what about a rule that was just like the original rule but with just one exception clause that permitted harvesting when conditions were exactly comparable to the stipulated conditions in our hypothetical example? Given that such a rule would even better maximize the good overall (a total of four more lives saved), act utilitarianism and rule utilitarianism would end up endorsing exactly the same requirement for our hypothetical example. Hence, rule utilitarianism would *not* be able to provide a way of constraining the imposition of irreparable harm on innocents that was desired.

Now suppose a defender of rule utilitarianism were to respond that it is just better to follow exceptionless rules even when doing so does not maximize the good overall. Is this an adequate defense? Recall that we were looking for a reason why we should not impose irreparable harm on innocent individuals even when it maximizes the good overall. Clearly, pointing out that maximizing the good overall in such examples would conflict with following an exceptionless rule does not seem to provide the grounds for rejecting such impositions for which we were looking. What is so good in and of itself about following exceptionless rules? At this point, defenders of rule utilitarianism tend to lapse into silence. There seems to be nothing more that can be said in defense of the view.

This means that we are still looking for a reason to reject impositions of irreparable harm on innocent individuals even when those impositions maximize the good overall. To begin to see what such a reason would be like, let us examine an obvious constraint on the requirement to maximize the good overall that virtually everyone accepts.

A BETTER DEFENSE: THE "OUGHT" IMPLIES "CAN" PRINCIPLE

Imagine that I were to fly through the air, like Superman, catch a small child as she is falling from her sixth-story apartment window, and restore her to the arms of her grateful parents. Surely that action, if I were to perform it, would be virtually guaranteed to maximize the good overall. Just the same, it is surely not something I am required to do, given that I clearly lack the physical powers of Superman to perform it. Similarly, what people ought to do has always been understood to be constrained by what they can or have the power to do. These constraints have been expressed in a principle known as "Ought" implies "Can."

Traditionally, this principle has also been thought to extend not to just what we are physically capable of doing, but to what we are logically and psychologically capable of doing as well. Clearly, if an action is logically or psychologically impossible for us to do, then it can't be an action that we ought to do—anymore than if an action is just physically impossible for us to do. Thus, this traditional "Ought" implies "Can" principle has always been accepted as a constraint on what we ought to do, and thus an independent constraint on any requirement we might have to maximize the good overall as well. Let us now see how this principle can also be plausibly extended beyond its usual reach.

Suppose you promised to attend a meeting on Friday, but on Thursday you're involved in a serious car accident, which leaves you in a coma. Surely it is no longer the case that you ought to attend the meeting now that you lack the power and thus are physically incapable of doing so. *Now here comes the extension.* Suppose instead that on Thursday you develop a severe case of pneumonia for which you are hospitalized. Although it would not, as in the previous case, be physically impossible for you to attend the meeting, surely you could legitimately claim that you *cannot* attend the meeting on the grounds that the risk to your health involved in attending is a sacrifice that in these circumstances, it would be unreasonable to require you to bear.

Thus, if sacrifices that are unreasonable to require us to bear give us legitimate grounds for not being required to perform certain acts, as they are widely thought to do, then we have another type of limitation on what we ought to do, similar to the constraints of the traditional "Ought" implies "Can" principle. Indeed, it is so similar to those constraints that we standardly convey it, as in the previous example, by saying that we *cannot* do such acts, just as we standardly say we *cannot* do acts that are logically, psychologically, or physically impossible for us to do. Accordingly, we have good reason to bring both of these restrictions together under the following expanded "Ought" implies "Can" principle:

> People are not morally required to do either what they lack the power to do or what would involve so great a sacrifice or restriction that it would be unreasonable to require them to perform such an action.

Now notice what happens when we apply this principle to our hypothetical case of the surgeon harvesting a healthy man's organs to save five terminally ill patients. In this case, the healthy man in no way caused the terminal illnesses of the five patients, and thus he is in no way responsible for them. Nor are a large number of lives at stake in this case. Rather, if the surgeon has her way, the healthy man's life will be sacrificed to save the lives of just five other people. While responsibility and numbers are relevant factors in such cases, in this particular case, neither comes into play. Of course, if our healthy man were willing to volunteer to sacrifice his life to save the five patients, that would be relevant. However, *I* have just now stipulated that the healthy man in our hypothetical case is *not* willing to volunteer. Accordingly, for our example, an expanded "Ought" implies "Can" principle would reject the forceful harvesting of a healthy man's organs as an unreasonable sacrifice, and hence, make it an action that morality cannot require, even if it did maximize the good overall. Happily, this is just the result we were looking for—an independent constraint on maximizing the good overall that limits the imposition of irreparable harm on innocent individuals.[10]

Nevertheless, although this expanded "Ought" implies "Can" principle will generally reject the imposition of irreparable harm on innocents to maximize the good overall, it will not always do so. The few cases where the principle will not reject such impositions will tend to be cases, similar to our spelunker example, where the imposition would be reasonable to require anyone affected to accept. We can see how this is so in the spelunker example because we can imagine all the spelunkers, the large person included, hypothetically agreeing beforehand that if one of them gets stuck in the mouth of the cave, a stick of dynamite should be used to blow that person out of the mouth of the cave. That hypothetical agreement serves to establish the reasonableness of the imposition in this and similar cases. Of course, in real-life cases, the application of an expanded "Ought" implies "Can" principle can be difficult to determine, but probably no more difficult to determine than what would maximize the good overall in such cases.

The obvious advantage of using this expanded "Ought" implies "Can" principle to limit the imposition of irreparable harm on innocents is that the principle is internal to utilitarian ethics itself. In fact, the principle is internal to all moral and political perspectives. The principle combines both the traditional "Ought" implies "Can" principle with a linkage between reason and morality that understands that the requirements of morality cannot impose unreasonable sacrifices on people. Given that both of these constraints are endorsed by all moral and political perspectives, their combination in this principle has to be endorsed as well.

Conclusion

We began this chapter entertaining the possibility that utilitarian ethics might have been useful to both Cheney and bin Laden. We considered the possibility that Cheney might have been able to use the view to defend torture and bin Laden to defend the terror of 9/11. We were led to the conclusion that while utilitarian ethics does, in principle, allow for the possibility of imposing irremediable harm on innocents to maximize the good overall, there are almost always, as a matter of fact, alternative ways of achieving the good overall that do not require such impositions on innocents. In fact, neither Cheney's use of torture nor bin Laden's use of terror was necessary to the achievement of their utilitarian goals.

While this realization was helpful, something was still lacking. While it was comforting that we were able to argue that, as a matter of fact, the use of torture or terror was not usually a necessary means to maximizing the good overall, what we really wanted was a reason for not imposing irremediable harm on innocents that was independent of maximizing the good overall.

At first, we looked to the distinction between act and rule utilitarianism for help since that distinction had been employed to try to provide a way to restrict the impositions of irremediable harm on innocents. Unfortunately, it turned out that the distinction was helpful only if we were attracted to the idea of following exceptionless rules for their own sake. That we should just follow exceptionless rules for their own sake, however, clearly does not appear to be the independent reason we are looking for to limit the imposing of irremediable harm on innocents.

Finally, we did find what we were looking for in an expanded "Ought" implies "Can" principle, a principle that, at least in its traditional form, we had already been using to constrain what we ought to do. We found that just as the traditional "Ought" implies "Can" principle rules out, as morally required, actions that we cannot do because they are logically, physically, or psychological impossible to do, so an expanded "Ought" implies "Can" principle, in addition, rules out actions that we cannot do because they are morally impossible to do. Actions are morally impossible to do when they would impose an unreasonable sacrifice on someone—something morality can never do.

At least since the time of Bentham and Mill, many moral philosophers have rejected utilitarian ethics because they thought that it easily justifies imposing irreparable harm on innocents to achieve a greater good overall. What we have seen in this chapter is that:

1. Once such impositions are evaluated against the alternatives, they often turn out, as matter of fact, not to be the way to maximize the good overall.
2. Once utilitarian ethics is seen to be internally constrained by an expanded "Ought" implies "Can" principle, still additional grounds present themselves for ruling out such impositions.

So interpreted, utilitarian ethics turns out to be a fairly attractive moral view.

MySearchLab Connections

Watch. Listen. Explore. Read. MySearchLab is designed just for you. Each chapter features a customized study plan to help you learn key concepts and terms. Dynamic visual activities, videos, and readings found in the multimedia library will enhance your learning experience.

Here are a few questions and activities to help you understand this chapter:

1. In what ways was Jeremy Bentham's utilitarianism influenced by earlier philosophers (p. 52)?

    Read "The History of Utilitarianism," Multimedia Library, Web Resources, Stanford Encyclopedia of Philosophy.

2. How did John Stuart Mill attempt to prove the Principle of Utility (p. 53)?

    Read "The History of Utilitarianism," Multimedia Library, Web Resources, Stanford Encyclopedia of Philosophy.

Each chapter features a customized study plan to help you learn and review key concepts and terms.

Notes

1. Jane Mayer, *The Dark Side* (New York: Doubleday, 2008), 9–10.
2. In the few statements by U.S. officials claiming that the United States ruled out the use of torture against detainees, the text made it clear that the CIA, at least, was exempt from this prohibition. See Mayer, *The Dark Side,* 125.

3. Bentham did, however, allow that pleasures could still be compared in terms of their intensity, duration, certainty, nearness, fruitfulness, and purity.

4. See Bybee Memo: http://www.tomjoad.org/bybeememo.htm.

5. Interestingly, the Bush lawyers claimed that even what constituted torture by their definition could be justified if the president authorized it.

6. The use of torture by the Bush Administration initially provided evidence for a link between Saddam Hussein and al-Qaeda, but later that evidence was discredited. See Mayer, *The Dark Side,* Chapter 6.

7. Catherine Lutz, "Research Cites 225,000 Lives Lost and US$4 Trillion in Spending on Post-9/11 Wars," Watson Institute, Brown University, June 28, 2011, http://www.watsoninstitute.org/news_detail.cfm?id=1536.

8. See Philippa Foot, "The Problem of Abortion and the Doctrine of Double Effect," *Oxford Review* 5 (1967), 5–15.

9. Mayer, *The Dark Side,* 104–106.

10. Of course, a defender of utilitarianism might consider rejecting this use of an expanded "Ought" implies "Can" principle to limit the imposition of irreparable harm on innocents in favor of an unconditional commitment to maximizing the good overall. Still, this use of an expanded "Ought" implies "Can" principle does provide a plausible way of eliminating what has historically been the strongest objection to utilitarian ethics.

CHAPTER 5

Kantian Ethics

One way to think about ethics that has often been taken to be opposed to the utilitarian ethics we discussed in Chapter 4 is expressed by the following challenge: *What if everyone did that?* For example, suppose you are considering cheating on your taxes, evading military service, or telling a small lie to advance your projects. How would you respond if challenged with the question, "What if everyone did that?"

Notice that the challenge is not that everyone else will act as you are proposing to act, and so the results of the combined acts of you and others would be disastrous. That would be a different argument—one based on the actual consequences of your actions and the actions of others—and it would not be a good argument because there is no reason to think that your action would be accompanied or followed by everyone else acting in exactly the same way. But that is not the argument that is being offered here. The argument that is being offered here is based not on what actually happens, but rather on what would happen if others acted as you are proposing to act.

Arguments of this sort historically draw on the work of Immanuel Kant (1724–1804). Born in Königsberg, East Prussia (now called Kaliningrad, and part of Russia), Kant never journeyed more than forty miles from the city. He was also so methodical that, according to legend, the citizens of Königsberg set their watches to his daily 3 p.m. walks. His works in ethics include *Foundations of a Metaphysics of Morals* (1786), *Critique of Practical Reason* (1790), and *Metaphysics of Morals* (1797).

KANT'S CATEGORICAL IMPERATIVE TEST

According to Kant, for our actions to be moral, they must be able to satisfy a certain test—a test that is somewhat similar to asking, "What if everyone did that?" Kant called his test the *Categorical Imperative*, and as he first formulates the test, it requires us to:

Act only on that maxim which you can at the same time will to be a universal law.[1]

To apply this test, when you are contemplating doing a particular act, you have to ask what rule you would be proposing to follow if you were to do that act. This is the "maxim of the act." To help explain how his test works, Kant gives the following example:

> Suppose I need to borrow money, and I know that no one will lend it to me unless I promise to repay the loan. But suppose I also know that I will not be able to repay. Should I therefore promise to repay the loan knowing that I will not be able to do so in order to persuade someone to loan the money to me?[2]

If I were to do that, the "maxim of my act" (the rule I would be following) would be: Whenever you need a loan, promise to repay it, regardless of whether you believe you actually will be able to do so.

Now could this rule become a universal law? Not if, as we are assuming in this case, everyone would know that, under these circumstances, people's promises were worthless. Because then no one would believe such promises, no one would make loans on the basis of them. As Kant himself puts it, "No one would believe what was promised to him but would only laugh at any such assertion as vain pretense."[3] So it would not be possible for a practice of lying promises to be sustained in such circumstances. As Kant sees it, making lying promises in these circumstances cannot satisfy his Categorical Imperative test.

In another example, Kant explains his test as follows:

> Suppose someone refused to help others in need, saying to herself, "What concern of mine is it? Let each one be happy as heaven wills ... but to his welfare or to his assistance in time of need I have no desire to contribute."[4]

Again, Kant claims this rule cannot be willed to be a universal law. For at some time in the future, Kant thinks that this person will surely find herself to be in need of assistance from others, and then she would not want others to be unconcerned about her. So, her commitment now not to help others in need, Kant thinks, would put her in conflict with what she would will later, assuming that she finds herself to be in need.

KANT, EGOISM AND HYPOTHETICAL IMPERATIVES

Kant also thinks that following maxims sanctioned by his Categorical Imperative test is a requirement of rationality as well as morality. However, egoists who are clearly opposed to morality can also be understood as acting according to a universal law, albeit a different universal law from the one followed by those committed to morality. For the egoist, the appropriate law is, *Everyone ought to do what best serves his or her own self-interest.* This principle of egoism seems in every way as ultimate and law-like as the Categorical Imperative and the maxims that satisfy its test.[5]

What distinguishes the requirements of egoism (self-interest), however, is their failure to pass Kant's Categorical Imperative test. While the egoist allows that others ought to do what best serves their own self-interest, she need not want or will that others do so, especially when that conflicts with what best serves the egoist's own self-interest. Seen in this way, there is nothing irrational about this behavior. In fact, as we noted in Chapter 3, this behavior parallels that of players in competitive games. In baseball, for example, a pitcher may think that the runner at first base ought to steal second while not wanting the runner to do so and indeed hoping to foil any attempt the runner makes. Since we do not regard the pitcher's behavior as irrational, no reason has been given for thinking that analogous behavior of the egoist is, in fact, irrational.

The egoist, however, would have no problem at all endorsing Kant's account of hypothetical imperatives. For Kant, hypothetical imperatives tell us what we ought to do provided we have the relevant desires. If you want a career in ballet, then you ought to commit yourself to practicing long hours. If you want to qualify for the Boston Marathon, then you ought to be running ten miles a day. The egoist has no problem at all accepting the conditional force of such hypothetical imperatives since they in no way conflict with the normative commitments of being an egoist. This is because anyone can always reject the relevant desires on which the normative force of the hypothetical imperatives depends. For example, if you no longer want a career in ballet, but now you want one in politics, certain hypothetical imperatives lose their normative force, while others acquire normative force. For the egoist, however, accepting the conditional normative force of hypothetical imperatives is perfectly consistent with rejecting the Categorical Imperative test as a requirement of rationality. The egoist, having her own way of universalizing, has not been shown to be irrational because she is not committed to universalizing as Kant's Categorical Imperative test requires.[6] Hence, if we want to defeat the egoist on grounds of rationality, we need to utilize the approach taken in Chapter 3.

A CENTRAL REQUIREMENT OF MORALITY

Yet meeting Kant's test does capture a central requirement of morality: its universalizability. What is morally required for me to do must be morally required for anyone else in my circumstances to do as well.[7] This means that moral requirements must not only satisfy the "Ought" implies "Can" principle and be logically, physically, and psychologically possible for me to do in my circumstances. It must be possible to universalize moral requirements, thus showing that everyone in my circumstances can do what I am doing.[8] This is just what Kant's test requires.

Nevertheless, maxims can meet Kant's test and still be morally defective. To see this, imagine a variant of Kant's lying promise example where the person's maxim is to make lying promises, but only when a sufficient number of other people, similarly situated, are not doing the same. Restricted in this way, the universalizing of one's lying would not negatively affect the general practice of promising because only a restricted number of people would be breaking their promises. Such a maxim would then pass Kant's Categorical Imperative test.

UNIVERSALIZABILITY NOT ENOUGH

Even so, there is a moral problem with such maxims. They go too far in allow-ing just anyone to break a promise as long as a sufficient number of other peo-ple are not doing the same. While exceptions to promise-keeping surely cannot be so numerous that they would have a negative impact on the practice, even hypothetically not having such an impact, as required by Kant's Categorical Imperative test, is not sufficient to justify making an exception of oneself. Mo-rality requires more; it requires that promise-breaking not impose unreasonable burdens on others and so it must be further limited to just those cases where people have the best reasons for breaking their promises. Simply claiming that my breaking my promises in a limited way, and others doing the same, would not have a negative impact on the practice of promise-making does not pro-vide sufficient justification for my promise-breaking. There must be some fur-ther reason that justifies my promise-breaking, but not the promise-breaking of others who are similarly situated. Thus, morality requires that the universaliz-ability of maxims be combined with adequate moral grounds for determining when exceptions are to be explicitly or implicitly included in those maxims.[9]

Moreover, the maxims that people employ in such cases could never be fully specified. Obviously, societal laws can never be fully specified to indicate all the present and future exceptions we should make to them. That is why we need courts to interpret our laws. But the same holds true for the promises and other agreements we make. They too can never be fully specified to indicate all the present and future exceptions we should make to them. In general, it is universalizability together with appropriate grounds for making exceptions that determines the morality that binds us in this regard.

Yet, just as Kant's Categorical Imperative universalizability test needed to be supplemented with adequate moral grounds for exceptions in order to prop-erly capture what we are morally required to do, something similar holds of the "What if everyone did that?" argument. It is not a sufficient moral test all by itself. The argument rightly indicates that moral requirements must be univer-salizable, and it further suggests that when everyone's acting as you do would lead to very bad consequences, your act would not be justified. The reason for this is not that these bad consequences would actually occur. Rather, it is that in acting in this way, you would be able to reap the benefits of your promise-breaking only because a sufficient number of other people, similarly situated, did not act as you did. What this shows is that absent some reason justifying your promise-breaking, but not theirs, your act of promise-breaking would not be morally justified because it would impose an unreasonable burden on oth-ers and thereby give you an unfair advantage.

OTHER FORMULATIONS OF KANT'S TEST

Not surprisingly, Kant, in two of his other formulations of the Categorical Im-perative, explicitly introduces further moral constraints on his universalizabil-ity test. In one formulation, Kant requires us to not treat people only as a means. He applies this formulation of his Categorical Imperative to his example of someone who wants to make a lying promise, claiming that to make such a promise treats the person to whom the promise is made as a means only. Yet, as we noted, if certain exceptions to keeping one's promises can be morally justified, then presumably doing so would involve showing appropriative regard to everyone affected and so not involve treating anyone as a means only.

Kant also thinks that people are used as a means only when "attempts on the freedom and property of others" are made.[10] While Kant does not make it clear when this occurs, contemporary libertarians often claim to be following Kant because of the importance they place on liberty and property.

In another formulation of his Categorical Imperative, Kant also requires that our universalized maxims must be acceptable to everyone in an idealized "kingdom of ends," where all are treated respectfully. Prominent twentieth-century philosopher, John Rawls, and his followers have worked to develop the normative standard suggested by this formulation of Kant's Categorical Imperative, but they have done so in a way that appears to conflict with a libertarian interpretation of Kantian ethics.

Thus, the moral constraints found in these other formulations of Kant's Categorical Imperative test do help to rule out problematic exceptions to universal practices that unfairly disadvantage some in order to benefit others. At the same time, they also imply seemingly divergent interpretations of Kantian ethics concerning how we should treat the poor or disadvantaged that requires a resolution in order for Kantian ethics to be of much practical use. So let us examine each of these interpretations in turn.

TWO INTERPRETATIONS OF KANT'S ETHICS

One of these interpretations of Kantian ethics endorses a welfare liberal (welfare and beyond) perspective with respect to the poor or disadvantaged, while the other interpretation endorses a libertarian (no welfare) perspective.

Welfare Liberalism

John Rawls is clearly the best-known defender of the welfare liberal perspective. In his widely acclaimed book, *A Theory of Justice*, Rawls argues that moral or just principles would emerge from an idealized choice situation—analogous to Kant's "kingdom of ends," where everyone is respected as an end in herself and not simply as a means. Yet Rawls goes beyond Kant by interpreting the conditions of his idealized choice situation to explicitly require a "veil of ignorance." This veil of ignorance, Rawls claims, requires that we discount certain knowledge about ourselves in order to reach fair agreements.

A good example of what is at issue here is the practice of withholding information from juries. As we know, judges sometimes refuse to allow juries to hear certain testimony. The rationale behind this practice is that certain information is highly prejudicial or irrelevant to the case at hand. The hope is that without this information, juries will be more likely to reach fair verdicts. Similarly, when prejudicial or irrelevant information is blurted out in the courtroom, intentionally or unintentionally, judges will usually instruct juries to discount that information, hoping to increase the likelihood that juries will reach fair verdicts. Of course, whether judges and juries in fact carry out their responsibilities in this regard is beside the point. What is crucial is that it is recognized in these contexts that justice demands that we discount certain information in order to achieve just results.

Rawls's idealized choice situation can be seen as simply a generalization of this practice. It maintains that if we are to achieve a fair system of rights and duties in general, then we must discount certain information about ourselves when choosing our system of rights and duties. In particular, we must discount our knowledge of whether we are rich or poor, talented or untalented, male or female or that we have a particular sexual orientation.[11] In general, this ideal of justice requires that we should choose as though we were standing behind an imaginary veil of ignorance with respect to most particular facts about ourselves, anything that would bias our choice or stand in the way of unanimous agreement. Rawls calls this choice situation "the original position" because it is the position we should start from when determining what fundamental rights and duties people should have.

It should be obvious that Rawls's original position is designed in such a way that it is virtually impossible for some kind of enforced welfare system not to be chosen. If Abigail is assuming that she doesn't know whether she is rich or poor, and she is deciding whether her society should have a tax-supported welfare system or not, surely she will want a welfare system. She would reason like this: If I turn out to be rich, I may be a bit unhappy that part of my wealth is taxed away to support the needy. But if I am poor and my society has no tax-supported welfare system, then without a considerable amount of charity, things could be very bad for me with my basic needs not being met. So choosing behind a veil of ignorance in Rawls's original position everyone would favor a tax-supported welfare system of some sort.

Nor would the welfare system that would be chosen in Rawls's original position be unconditional. Recall Aesop's fable of the grasshopper and the ant. Throughout the summer, the grasshopper enjoyed himself, refusing to store up food for the coming winter, while the ant worked hard to do just that. With the approach of winter, the grasshopper pleaded with the ant for help but the ant refused, reminding the grasshopper that he had done nothing to store up food for himself when he had the chance to do so. Similarly, persons in Rawls's original position would favor making their tax-supported welfare system conditional on the poor first doing what they legitimately can do to help themselves. Even if they turned out to be in a position analogous to that of the grasshopper in Aesop's fable, persons in Rawls's original position would reason they would not be justified in forcefully getting others to help them. Nevertheless, while one Kantian-inspired ethical view is thus said to lead to a tax-supported welfare system, another view, reflecting another part of Kant's theory, is said to lead to a rejection of just such a system.

Libertarianism

Accordingly, contemporary libertarians see themselves as defenders of an ideal of liberty that has Kantian roots and avoids treating people as means only. Austrian-born philosopher and economist F. A. Hayek, who received a Nobel

Prize in economics, is probably the most well-known contemporary libertarian. Hayek saw his work as restating an ideal of liberty for our times, "We are concerned with that condition of men in which coercion of some by others is reduced as much as possible in society."[12] Similarly, American philosopher and Libertarian Party presidential candidate, John Hospers believes that libertarianism is "a philosophy of personal liberty—the liberty of each person to live according to his own choices, provided that he does not attempt to coerce others and thus prevent them from living according to their choices."[13] And contemporary philosopher, Robert Nozick claims that if a moral view goes beyond libertarian side-constraints that only prohibit interference, it cannot avoid the prospect of continually interfering with people's lives.

Taking liberty as the absence of interference by other people from doing what they otherwise either want or are just able to do, libertarians go on to characterize their political ideal as requiring that each person should have the greatest amount of liberty morally commensurate with the greatest amount of liberty for everyone else. Interpreting their ideal in this way, libertarians claim to derive a number of more specific requirements, in particular, a right to life; a right to freedom of speech, press, and assembly; and a right to property.

Here it is important to observe that the libertarian's right to life is not a right to receive from others the goods and resources necessary for preserving one's life; it is simply a right not to have one's life interfered with or ended unjustly. Correspondingly, the libertarian's right to property is not a right to receive from others the goods and resources necessary for one's welfare, but rather typically a right not to be interfered with in regard to any goods and resources that one has legitimately acquired either by initial acquisition or by voluntary agreement.[14]

SUPPORTING EXAMPLES

In support of their view, libertarians have advanced examples of the following sort. The first two are adapted from American economist and Nobel laureate Milton Friedman, the last from Robert Nozick.

In the first example, you are to suppose you and three friends are walking along the street and you happen to notice and retrieve a $100 bill lying on the pavement. Imagine a rich fellow had passed by earlier throwing away $100 bills, and you have been lucky enough to find one of them. According to Friedman, it would be nice of you to share your good fortune with your friends. Nevertheless, they have no right to demand that you do so, and hence, they would not be justified in forcing you to share the $100 bill with them. Similarly, Friedman would have us believe that it would be nice of us to provide welfare to the less fortunate members of our society. Nevertheless, the less fortunate members have no right to welfare, and hence they would not be justified in forcing us to provide such.

The second example, which Friedman regards as analogous to the first, involves supposing that there are four Robinson Crusoes, each marooned on four uninhabited islands in the same neighborhood. One of these Crusoes happens to land on a large and fruitful island, which enables him to live easily and well. The others happen to land on tiny and rather barren islands from which they can barely scratch out a living. Suppose one day they discover the existence of each other. Now, according to Friedman, it would be nice of the fortunate Robinson Crusoe to share the resources of his island with the other three Crusoes, but the other three Crusoes have no right to demand that he share those resources, and it would be wrong of them to force him to do so. Correspondingly, Friedman thinks it would be nice of us to provide the less fortunate in our society with welfare, but the less fortunate have no right to demand that we do so, and it would be wrong of them to force us to do so.

In the third example, Robert Nozick asks us to imagine that we are in a society that has just distributed income according to some ideal pattern, possibly a pattern of equality. We are further to imagine that in such a society someone with the athletic talents of Kobe Bryant offers to play basketball for us provided that he receives, let us say, $10 from every home game ticket that is sold. Suppose we agree to these terms, and 2 million people attend the home games to see Bryant play, thereby securing for him an income of $20 million. Since such an income would surely upset the initial pattern of income distribution, whatever that happened to be, Nozick contends that this illustrates how an ideal of liberty upsets the patterns required by other conceptions of justice, and hence calls for their rejection.

Of course, libertarians allow that it would be nice of the rich to share their surplus goods and resources with the poor, just as Milton Friedman would allow that it would be nice of you to share the $100 you found with your friends, and nice of the rich-islanded Robinson Crusoe to share his resources with the poor-islanded Robinson Crusoes. Nevertheless, they deny that government has a duty to provide for such needs. Some good things, such as providing welfare to the poor, are requirements of charity rather than justice, libertarians claim. Accordingly, failure to make such provisions is neither blameworthy nor punishable. As a consequence, such acts of charity should not be coercively required. For this reason, libertarians are opposed to tax-supported welfare programs.

So Kant's ethical theory has given rise to two seemingly divergent perspectives in contemporary ethics, a welfare liberal perspective that supports the right to welfare and a libertarian perspective that rejects any such right. The welfare liberal perspective appeals to an ideal of fairness found in Kant's view to support its right to welfare. The libertarian perspective appeals to an ideal of liberty also found in Kant's view to reject such a right.

Is it then possible to argue in some nonquestion-begging way that an ideal of fairness has moral priority over an ideal of liberty, or vice versa? It is not clear how one would do this. Alternatively, is there then some more general moral ideal—such as an ideal of respect—that can be shown to favor one of these two ideals over the other? Again, it is not clear how one would show this. For example, both ideals of fairness and liberty can be legitimately construed to be interpretations of the more general ideal of respect, which, therefore, cannot be used to choose between them.

At this point, some contemporary philosophers, notably contemporary philosopher Alasdair MacIntyre, have argued that we are facing here incommensurable ideals with no nonarbitrary way of choosing between them. Still, there may be a reasonable way of making a choice in this particular case. Suppose the libertarian ideal of liberty could be shown to support the same right to welfare that is supported by the welfare liberal ideal of fairness. Surely, this would be a welcomed resolution of the conflict between these two seemingly different Kantian ideals. Yet could libertarians really be mistaken about what their ideal of liberty requires?

CONFLICTING LIBERTIES

In order to see if this is the case, consider a typical conflict situation between the rich and the poor. In this conflict situation, the rich, of course, have more than enough resources to satisfy their basic needs.[15] In contrast, imagine that the poor lack the resources to meet their basic needs so as to secure a decent life for themselves, even though they have tried all the means available to them that libertarians regard as legitimate for acquiring such resources. Under circumstances like these, libertarians maintain that the rich should have the liberty to use their resources to satisfy their luxury needs if they so wish. Libertarians recognize that this liberty might well be enjoyed with the consequence that the satisfaction of the basic needs of the poor will not be met; they just think that liberty always has priority over other political ideals, and since they assume that the liberty of the poor is not at stake in such conflict situations, it is easy for them to conclude that the rich should not be required to sacrifice their liberty so that the basic needs of the poor may be met.

Of course, libertarians allow that it would be nice of the rich to share their surplus resources with the poor. Nevertheless, according to libertarians, such acts of charity are not required because the liberty of the poor is not thought to be at stake in such conflict situations. In fact, however, the liberty of the poor is at stake in such conflict situations. What is at stake is the liberty of the poor not to be interfered with in taking from the surplus possessions of the rich what is necessary to satisfy their basic needs.

Now when the conflict between the rich and the poor is viewed as a conflict of liberties, either we can say that the rich should have the liberty not to be interfered with in using their surplus resources for luxury purposes, or we can say that the poor should have the liberty not to be interfered with in taking from the rich what they require to meet their basic needs. If we choose one liberty, we must reject the other. What needs to be determined, therefore, is which liberty is morally enforceable: the liberty of the rich or the liberty of the poor.[16]

An Expanded "Ought" Implies "Can" Principle Again

Now to see why the liberty of the poor, understood as the liberty not to be interfered with when taking from the surplus resources of others what is required to meet one's basic needs, is morally preferable to the liberty of the rich, understood as the liberty not to be interfered with when using one's surplus resources for luxury purposes, we need only appeal again, as we did in interpreting utilitarianism, to an expanded "Ought" implies "Can" principle. This principle combines the traditional "Ought" implies "Can" principle with the widespread conviction that morality cannot impose unreasonable requirements on anyone. According to the principle, people are not morally required to do either what they lack the power to do or what would involve so great a sacrifice or restriction that it would be unreasonable to require them to perform such an action.

Now applying this expanded "Ought" implies "Can" principle to the case at hand, it seems clear that the poor have it within their power to relinquish such an important liberty as the liberty not to be interfered with when taking from the rich what they require to meet their basic needs. They could do this. Nevertheless, it is unreasonable in this context to require them to accept so great a restriction. In the extreme case, it involves requiring the poor to sit back and starve to death. Of course, the poor may have no real alternative to relinquishing this liberty. To do anything else may involve worse consequences for themselves and their loved ones and may invite a painful death. Accordingly, we may expect that the poor would accede, albeit unwillingly, to a political system that denied them the right to welfare supported by such a liberty, at the same time we recognize that such a system has imposed an unreasonable restriction upon the poor—a restriction that we could not morally blame the poor for trying to evade. Analogously, we might expect that a woman whose life is threatened would submit to a rapist's demands, at the same time that we recognize the utter unreasonableness of those demands.

By contrast, it is not unreasonable to require the rich in this context to sacrifice the liberty to meet some of their luxury needs so that the poor can have the liberty to meet their basic needs. Naturally, we might expect that the rich, for reasons of self-interest or past contribution, might be disinclined to make such a sacrifice. We might even suppose that the past contributions of the rich provide a good reason for not sacrificing their liberty to use their surplus for luxury purposes. Yet, the rich cannot claim that relinquishing such a liberty involves so great a sacrifice that it is unreasonable to require them to make it. So it is the rich here, and not the poor, who are morally blameworthy and subject to coercion for failing to make the appropriate sacrifice.

Consequently, if we assume that however else we specify the requirements of morality, they cannot violate an expanded "Ought" implies "Can" principle, it follows that, despite what libertarians claim, the right to liberty endorsed by them actually favors the liberty of the poor over the liberty of the rich.

Libertarian Objections

Yet couldn't libertarians object to this conclusion, claiming that it would be unreasonable to require the rich to sacrifice the liberty to meet some of their luxury needs so that the poor can have the liberty to meet their basic needs? As I have pointed out, libertarians don't usually see the situation as a conflict of liberties, but suppose they did. How plausible would such an objection be?

Consider: What are libertarians going to say about the poor? Isn't it clearly unreasonable to require the poor to restrict their liberty to meet their basic needs so that the rich can have the liberty to meet their luxury needs? Isn't it clearly unreasonable to coercively require the poor to sit back and starve to death? If so, no resolution of this conflict is reasonable to coercively require both the rich and the poor to accept. But that would mean that libertarians could not be putting forth a moral resolution because a moral resolution, according to an expanded "Ought" implies "Can" principle, resolves severe conflicts of interest in ways reasonable to require everyone affected to accept, where it is further understood that a moral resolution can sometimes require us to act in accord with altruistic reasons. Therefore, as long as libertarians think of themselves as putting forth a moral resolution, they cannot allow that it is unreasonable in cases of severe conflict of interest both to require the rich to restrict their liberty to meet their luxury needs in order to benefit the poor and to require the poor to restrict their liberty to meet their basic needs in order to benefit the rich. But if one of these requirements is to be judged reasonable, then, by any neutral assessment, it must be the requirement that the rich restrict their liberty to meet their luxury needs so that the poor can have the liberty to meet their basic needs. There is no other plausible resolution, if libertarians intend to put forth a moral resolution.

Now it might also be objected that the right to welfare that this argument establishes from libertarian premises is not the same as the right to welfare endorsed by welfare liberals and socialists. This is correct. We could mark this difference by referring to the right that this argument establishes as "a negative welfare right" and by referring to the right endorsed by welfare liberals as "a positive welfare right." The significance of this difference is that a person's negative welfare right can be violated only when other people, through acts of commission, interfere with its exercise, whereas a person's positive welfare right can be violated not only by such acts of commission but by acts of omission as well. For example, just letting the poor starve to death (an act of omission but not one of commission) would not violate the poor's negative right to welfare but it would violate the poor's positive right to welfare if they had one.

Nonetheless, this difference will have little practical import because in recognizing the legitimacy of negative welfare rights, libertarians will come to see that virtually any use of their surplus possessions is likely to violate the negative welfare rights of the poor by preventing the poor from rightfully appropriating (some part of) their surplus goods and resources. So, in order to ensure that they will not be engaging in such wrongful actions, it will be incumbent on them to set up institutions guaranteeing adequate positive welfare rights for the poor. Only then will they be able to use legitimately any remaining surplus possessions to meet their own nonbasic needs. Furthermore, in the absence of adequate positive welfare rights, the poor, either acting by themselves or through their allies or agents, would have some discretion in determining when and how to exercise their negative welfare rights. In order not to be subject to that discretion, libertarians will tend to favor the only morally legitimate way of preventing the exercise of such rights: They will set up institutions guaranteeing adequate positive welfare rights that will then take precedence over the exercise of negative welfare rights. For these reasons, recognizing the negative welfare rights of the poor will ultimately lead libertarians to endorse the same sort of welfare institutions favored by welfare liberals.

Conclusion

Our understanding of how to interpret Kant's ethics has changed over time. Most philosophers today no longer think that Kant's Categorical Imperative defeats the egoist. Most also recognize that the Categorical Imperative test needs to be supplemented with appropriate moral grounds for making exceptions. We have also seen how Kantian ethics with its two competing interpretations of welfare liberalism and libertarianism can be reconciled in practice. This practical reconciliation should also help to reconcile Kantian and utilitarian ethics once we take into account that both views are significantly morally constrained by the same expanded "Ought" implies "Can" principle. This is because whether we are weighing people's interests, as in utilitarian ethics, or their liberties, as in Kantian ethics, what matters most is that the weighing be constrained by an expanded "Ought" implies "Can" principle so that unreasonable sacrifices are not imposed on anyone.

MySearchLab Connections

Watch. Listen. Explore. Read. MySearchLab is designed just for you. Each chapter features a customized study plan to help you learn key concepts and terms. Dynamic visual activities, videos, and readings found in the multimedia library will enhance your learning experience.

Here are a few questions and activities to help you understand this chapter:

1. In what ways was Immanuel Kant's ethics a response to the views of David Hume (p. 65)?

   📖 Read "Kant and Hume on Morality," Multimedia Library, Web Resources, Stanford Encyclopedia of Philosophy.

2. How did Kant's ethics influence the work of John Rawls's attempt to prove the Principle of Utility (p. 69)?

   📖 Read "John Rawls," Multimedia Library, Web Resources, Internet Encyclopedia of Philosophy.

Each chapter features a customized study plan to help you learn and review key concepts and terms.

Notes

1. Immanuel Kant, *Foundations of the Metaphysics of Morals*, trans. Lewis Beck (Indianapolis: Bobbs-Merrill, 1959), 422.

2. Ibid., 423.

3. Ibid.

4. Ibid., 424.

5. Kant further contrasts morality with self-interest by characterizing morality as unconditionally binding (independent of what we happen to desire). For example, our obligation to keep our promises is usually understood to be binding whether we desire to keep our promises. But the same holds true of self-interest. What is really in our self-interest, or really for our own good, is also binding, independent of what we happen to desire. As the majority of cigarette smokers can surely attest, what is truly in their interest is often contrary to the persistent desires they have to smoke. Accordingly, the requirements of morality cannot be claimed to be rationally required over those of self-interest on the grounds that they are unconditional (independent of what we happen to desire), whereas the requirements of self-interest are not.

6. Nor would the egoist accept the Kantian view that the only thing good without qualification is a good will, that is, a morally good will, unless Kant was successful in showing that the Categorical Imperative is a requirement of rationality, just what the egoist denies. Without such an argument, the egoist would probably regard Kant's good will as something that is in her interest that others have, but not something that is in her interest that she herself should have. That way the egoist would be able to consistently take unfair advantage of others having a good will.

7. "My circumstances" here can include abilities or characteristics that I just happen to have, like being able to swim fast enough to save someone from drowning.

8. Egoism makes no assumption that we all can do what we egoistically ought to do together, but neither does the "oughts" of competitive games. Yet neither should be judged irrational on that account.

9. The perceptive reader will note that the reasons why Kant's universalizability test by itself, as initially formulated, is not an adequate moral standard parallel the reasons why rule utilitarianism by itself is not an adequate moral standard.

10. Kant, *Foundations of the Metaphysics of Morals*, 430.

11. Rawls doesn't mention sexual orientation as one of our characteristics of which we should imagine ourselves to be ignorant, but if unfairness is to be avoided, it should be included.

12. F. A. Hayek, *The Constitution of Liberty* (Chicago: University of Chicago Press, 1960), 11.

13. John Hospers, *Libertarianism* (Los Angeles: Nash Publishing, 1971), 5.

14. Property can also be legitimately acquired on the libertarian view by producing it out of what one already owns or legitimately possesses.

15. Basic needs, if not satisfied, lead to significant lacks or deficiencies with respect to a standard of mental and physical well-being. Thus, a person's needs for food, shelter, medical care, protection, companionship, and self-development are, at least in part, needs of this sort. For a discussion of basic needs, see James P. Sterba, *How to Make People Just* (Lanham, MD: Rowman and Littlefield, 1988), 45–48.

16. Libertarians have never rejected the need for enforcement when important liberties are at stake.

CHAPTER 6

Aristotelian Ethics

W hat do you want to be when you grow up? This simple question that we were all asked many times when we were children suggests yet another way of thinking about ethics—as a way of *being* rather than as a way of *acting*. This way of thinking about ethics, contrasting some-what with both utilitarian and Kantian ethics, has its historical roots in ancient Greece, particularly in the work of Aristotle (384–322 BC).

Born in the northern Greek city of Stagira in Macedonia, Aristotle entered Plato's Academy when he was eighteen and studied and taught there for approximately twenty years. Plato is said to have considered him "the mind" of the Academy. Nevertheless, in his will, Plato named his nephew Speusip-pus head of the Academy rather than his gifted student Aristotle. So Aristotle left Athens and went to Assos in Asia Minor where he established a branch campus of the Academy. In 343 BC, Philip of Macedon invited Aristotle to tutor his thirteen-year-old son, Alexander, who was to become Alexander the Great. Soon after the death of Philip, Aristotle returned to Athens and began his own school, the Lyceum, where he produced most of the works that survive to this day in the form of lecture notes.

HAPPINESS AND THE VIRTUOUS LIFE

In one of his most famous works, the *Nicomachean Ethics*, named after his son who is supposed to have edited these notes, Aristotle attempts to provide eth-ics with a firm foundation. He begins by noting that all human activity aims at some good. He then argues that, for humans, happiness is the ultimate good, but that happiness is wrongly thought to consist simply in pleasure, wealth, and honor. Rightly understood, Aristotle argues, happiness for humans requires a virtuous life. So the proper goal for humans is to be virtuous. Thus, ethics is primarily specified as a way of *being* rather than as a way of *acting*, although the two are obviously connected since being virtuous will obviously require acting in certain ways on certain occasions.

Nevertheless, this identification of the virtuous life and happiness does raise a problem for Aristotle and for contemporary Aristotelians because it is not clear how the two things can or should be identified. Thus, imagine that you are engaged in the following dialogue with Aristotle:

YOU: Why should I be virtuous?

A: Well, we agree, don't we, that it is a good thing to be happy?

YOU: Suppose we do.

A: It turns out that being virtuous is necessary to make you happy. So that is why you should be virtuous.

YOU: But according to the ordinary notion of happiness, it seems possible to be happy without always being virtuous.

A: But as I define happiness, being happy requires being virtuous.

YOU: But then doesn't my original question return in a different form? Why should I seek happiness in your sense and thereby always be virtuous rather than seek happiness in the ordinary sense and only sometimes be virtuous?

A: That is an interesting objection.

Of course, Aristotle never did give up on the necessity of virtue for happiness. Yet he did, unlike Plato, hold that certain external goods, like health, adequate wealth, and good fortune, are also necessary for happiness. Contemporary Aristotelians have tended to deal with the challenge to the necessity of virtue for happiness by simply focusing on the proper characterization of a virtuous life, and setting the challenge aside to be dealt with later.

According to Aristotle, a virtue is a desirable trait of character that is a mean between two vices, one of excess and the other of deficiency. Courage, for example, is a mean between the vices of foolhardiness and cowardice. Aristotle also distinguishes between intellectual and moral virtues. Intellectual virtues can be taught like logic and mathematics. By contrast, moral virtues, such as benevolence, honesty, loyalty, consciousness, and patience, can be learned only through practice. As Aristotle puts it,

> Men become builders by building and lyre players by playing the lyre so too we become just by doing just acts, temperate by doing temperate acts, brave by doing brave acts.[1]

Aristotle uses the virtue of courage to further illustrate how a moral virtue is a mean between two vices, one of excess and the other of deficiency. Courage, when examined more closely, has two components: fear and confidence. As a consequence, we can err in regard to either factor by having too much or too little fear, or too much or too little confidence. If we have too little fear or too much confidence, we display the vice of foolhardiness. If we have too much fear or too little confidence, we display the opposing vice of cowardice.

Nevertheless, Aristotle thinks that his mean analysis of virtue doesn't work for all cases. To demonstrate this, he gives the example of murder as an action that is always wrong and does not admit of a mean. But regarding murder as always wrong does not seem to conflict with Aristotle's analysis of virtue. The relevant virtue here, which is a mean, can be called respect for the lives of others. Murder would then be one way of displaying the vice of too little respect for the lives of others. The contrasting vice would be that of showing too much respect for the lives of others. This would involve being unduly willing to sacrifice one's own life for others, especially in cases where such sacrifice is not really needed or deserved. As further support for Aristotle's analysis, we might also think of virtue generally either as a mean between favoring our own interests too much or too little or as a mean between favoring the interests of others too much or too little.[2]

It was also part of Aristotle's view that the ability of people to be virtuous is vastly unequal. As Aristotle saw it, some men were natural slaves and all women lacked the full capacity to reason. As a consequence, both groups were naturally destined to be ruled by free men. Happily, contemporary Aristotelians, benefiting from further reflection on the relevant data, have chosen not to follow Aristotle in this regard.

CHARACTERIZING THE VIRTUOUS LIFE

Even so, it is not easy to properly characterize a virtuous life. Contemporary philosopher Alasdair MacIntyre attempts to characterize it in terms of practices that have goods that are internal and external to them.[3] In basketball, for example, a good internal to the practice would be the pleasure that comes from coordinated play with your teammates, while a good external to the practice would be the cheers you happen to receive from those watching you play. Yet while MacIntyre's connection of a virtuous life to practices is helpful, he does not go on to determine which practices constitute a virtuous life and which do not, and unfortunately this leaves the concept of a virtuous life open to a multitude of different and possibly conflicting interpretations.

Another contemporary philosopher, Martha Nussbaum, tries to do better. She defines virtue as being disposed to choose and respond well in the eight important spheres of shared human experience, which are as follows:[4]

- mortality,
- the body,
- pleasure and pain,
- cognitive ability,
- practical reason,
- early infant development,
- affiliation, and
- humor.

With respect to each of these spheres, Nussbaum claims that relevant virtues can be specified in an objective, nonrelativist way. While this does add more detail to an account of a virtuous life, it still leaves many questions unresolved. In particular, it leaves open the question of whether a virtuous concern with these spheres of human experience is centered on just one's own good (happiness) or whether it also takes into account the good (happiness) of others. As we have seen, Aristotle's linkage of the virtuous life with one's own happiness might seem to favor the first interpretation. Yet at least some contemporary Aristotelians, notably contemporary philosophers, Julia Annas and Robert Adams, favor an account of a virtuous life that includes a strong concern for the good of others as well as for one's own good.[5] Such an interpretation of Aristotelian ethics would also make the view more similar to Kantian and utilitarian ethics, both of which have a strong other-regarding focus. In turn, it should lead to consideration of distant peoples and future generations within Aristotelian ethics, given that these other-regarding concerns are also taken up in Kantian and utilitarian ethics.

CONFLICTS WITH KANTIAN ETHICS

Even if some degree of reconciliation is possible, Kantian and Aristotelian ethics, in particular, have been thought to clash significantly over the ideal of a virtuous person. Consider the following. In his *Nicomachean Ethics*, Aristotle draws a distinction between a "fully virtuous" person, let's call her Angel, who acts virtuously and in accordance with her desires, and a "self-controlled" person, let's call her Stoa, who also acts virtuously but against her desires. By contrast, Kant, in his *Groundwork of a Metaphysics of Morals*, uses two examples to help elucidate his ideal of a virtuous person. The first example is that of a person, let's call her Angelina, who finds it very easy and attractive to act according to duty but whose actions, Kant claims, are not fully virtuous because she does not act from a sense of duty. The second example is that of a person, let's call her Stoalina, who is naturally cold-hearted, but whose actions, Kant claims, are virtuous because she manages to help others out of a sense of duty. Now while Angel is similar to Angelina and Stoa is similar to Stoalina, Aristotle clearly prefers Angel to Stoa, while Kant clearly prefers Stoalina to Angelina. So it would appear that Kant and Aristotle are radically disagreeing over who is a virtuous person. The person who Kant takes to be the more virtuous seems to be less virtuous for Aristotle, and the person who Aristotle takes to be the more virtuous seems to be the less virtuous for Kant.

As some contemporary Aristotelians and Kantians have shown, however, there are good reasons to both agree and disagree with Kant's and Aristotle's views in this regard.[6] First, in support of Kant's view but not Aristotle's, there surely are cases where the harder it is for a person to act virtuously the more virtuous the person is. For example, some soldiers may have to struggle against great odds to defend a military position from attack, while others do their military duty safely behind the lines. In such cases, the harder it is for the person to act virtuously, the greater the virtue. Second, in support of Aristotle's view but not Kant's, failing to be naturally inclined to perform certain virtuous acts can tell against one's virtue. The naturally cold-hearted person in Kant's example who helps the poor but only from duty is clearly not as virtuous as someone who helps the poor motivated both by duty and by a heartfelt sympathy for the poor. Third, with respect to Kant's case where people find it easy to act according to duty but where their motivation is not virtuous at all, as when shopkeepers treat their customers honestly but only because it is good for business, Aristotle would not disagree because he too required the virtuous person to be appropriately motivated. So it turns out that not only are the best elements of Aristotle's and Kant's accounts of a virtuous person not radically opposed, but they also need to be combined into one unified account if we want to have the most morally defensible view.

THE IMPORTANCE OF RULES

Another area of opposition between Aristotelians and Kantians has been over the importance of rules to morality. Some Aristotelians have noted how difficult it is to devise relevant rules with respect to many of the virtues of ordinary life.[7] Consider the virtues of gratitude and self-respect. It is difficult to know how we could specify rules relevant to these virtues except by using the uninformative admonitions "Be grateful" and "Respect yourself." We surely cannot specify what is required in such a way, for example, that an ungrateful person could still obey the relevant rule with respect to gratitude while lacking the appropriate motives and beliefs required for exercising that virtue. Obeying rules of this sort requires more than just some external conduct; it requires having certain relevant intentions and beliefs as well. So, for many of the virtues of ordinary life, rules turn out not to be very useful for communicating what should be done. What are generally more helpful to communicating what should be done are stories or paradigm cases of virtuous action, such as the story of the Good Samaritan.

Now while it is usually Aristotelians who make these points about the limitations of rules, it is not clear why Kantians or utilitarians need deny anything that Aristotelians are claiming here. Kantians and utilitarians can grant that with respect to many of the virtues of ordinary life, there is no corresponding rule that is useful in communicating what should be done. At the same time, they can point out that with respect to other virtues of ordinary life, there are more useful and more informative rules. For example, for truthfulness "Don't lie," for honesty, "Don't steal," and for respect for innocent life, "Don't kill." The reason why these rules are a bit more useful and more informative is that they provide an alternative way of characterizing what their respective virtues require. Of course, Aristotelians need not deny that this is the case, and this should lead to considerable agreement between Kantians and Aristotelians concerning both the limitations and the usefulness of moral rules.[8]

FOCUSING ON HOW WE SHOULD ACT

The focus of Aristotelian ethics on a way of being must be taken into account in any adequate theory of ethics. On any given occasion, a person's character, intentions, and actions can all be subject to independent moral evaluation. A negative evaluation of any one of these features of human agency does not necessarily entail a negative evaluation of the others. Nor does a positive evaluation of any one of these features necessarily entail a positive evaluation of the others. For example, one could have inadvertently caused considerable harm to others (have acted badly) even though one meant well (had good intentions) or was characteristically benevolent (had a good character). Alternatively, to use an example from contemporary philosopher Robert Merrihew Adams, one could be somewhat timid (have a weak character) yet mean well (have good intentions), but as a consequence miss an opportunity for an enriching life experience (without having acted badly). That is why a morally adequate theory of ethics must concern itself with all three of these features of human agency.

While Aristotelian ethics is celebrated for its focus on character and intentions (how we should be) rather than actions (how we should act), philosopher Rosalind Hursthouse of New Zealand has sought to show that Aristotelian ethics can still tell us how we should act. According to Hursthouse, right action is what a virtuous agent would do in the circumstances.[9] Sometimes this standard is interpreted to require doing what a perfectly virtuous agent would do in the circumstances—some would say what Jesus, Gandhi, or Muhammad would do in the circumstances. But this may not be the best way to interpret the standard because it may be impossible for a perfectly virtuous agent to actually be in the particular circumstances in which we find ourselves.

More usefully, Aristotle compares the process through which a person learns to be virtuous to the process by which a person learns to play a harp.[10] At each stage, what a person should do is not what a completely virtuous person (or fully expert harpist) does, but rather what a person at one's particular stage of development should do next to become more virtuous (or a better harpist). In the pursuit of virtue, the stage one is presently at, could, for example, involve a grossly immoral lifestyle, and so it would not make sense to ask what a perfectly virtuous agent would do in such circumstances because, of course, a perfectly virtuous agent would never be in such circumstances. In fact, no virtuous agent would ever be in such circumstances. Still, if you happen to find yourself in such circumstances, you can always ask yourself what would be the next step you should take to morally improve your character.

THE PRIORITY QUESTION

Now consider circumstances that are compatible with the existence of a morally virtuous agent. In such circumstances, do the choices of morally virtuous agents actually determine the rightness of acts? Consider an act of saving a child from drowning. Isn't the primary reason this act is right that it would save the child's life, rather than that a morally virtuous agent (with the requisite life-saving abilities) would choose to perform that act? If anything, the rightness of the act would seem to explain why a morally virtuous person would choose to perform it.

Does this mean that utilitarian and Kantian ethics with their focus on ethics as a way of acting have an advantage over Aristotelian ethics with its focus on ethics as a way of being? Not necessarily.[11] There are other examples where the rightness or wrongness of an action is far less clear and for which the best way to determine what to do is to consider what an ideally virtuous person, such as Socrates, Joan of Arc, Martin Luther King, Jr., or even your own uncle Bill or aunt Natasha, would do in such circumstances.

For example, imagine you are trying to decide what to do with your life. Surely, considering what ideally virtuous agents with your abilities would choose to do can help you answer this question. Even utilitarians and Kantians recognize the usefulness of appealing to what ideally virtuous agents would choose to do in determining what is right and wrong. For example, utilitarian ethics appeals to what an ideally sympathetic agent would choose and Kantian ethics appeals to what ideally rational people in the kingdom of ends would choose. It would seem best, therefore, not to assign a priority to any of the three ethical perspectives in this regard.

Moreover, it also seems appropriate to regard Aristotelian ethics, just like utilitarian and Kantian ethics, to be constrained by an expanded "Ought" implies "Can" principle that joins together the traditional "Ought" implies "Can" principle with the widespread conviction that morality cannot impose unreasonable requirements on anyone. So interpreted, the three ethical perspectives would appear to lead to similar practical requirements. This would particularly appear to be the case if a concern for the good of others as well as oneself is taken to be part of a virtuous life, and if all people, including distant peoples as well as future generations, are understood to be part of that concern.

AYN RAND'S ARISTOTELIAN ETHICS

Nevertheless, there is another very popular interpretation of Aristotelian ethics that seems strongly opposed to most contemporary interpretations of Kantian and utilitarian ethics, and so would be against any kind of practical reconciliation with those views. This interpretation is found in the work of novelist/philosopher Ayn Rand. Given that her work provides us with an interpretation of Aristotelian ethics that is strongly opposed to most contemporary interpretations of Kantian and utilitarian ethics, it clearly deserves our attention.

Ayn Rand (Alice Rosenbaum) was born in St. Petersburg, Russia, in 1905. Her most successful novels were *The Fountainhead* (1943), which was made into a movie starring Gary Cooper and Patricia Neal, and *Atlas Shrugged* (1957), both of which have sold millions of copies. Rand also published a number of works of nonfiction such as *The Virtue of Selfishness* (1964) that more directly set out her version of Aristotelian ethics.

Regarding Aristotle as the greatest of all philosophers, Rand draws on his view to develop a virtue theory of selfishness in which the primary moral requirement is to be concerned with one's own interests. She sees her theory as opposed to an altruism that regards any action done for the benefit of others as good and any action done for one's own benefit as evil.[12] According to Rand,

> ... every human being is an end in himself, not the means to the ends or welfare of others—and, therefore, that man must live for his own sake, neither sacrificing himself to others, nor sacrificing others to himself. To live for his own sake means that the achievement of his own happiness is man's highest moral purpose.[13]

Unfortunately, Rand's characterization of altruism here is a bit overdrawn as a critique of utilitarian and Kantian ethics. Neither of these views regards as *evil* any action done for one's own benefit. Rather, both views simply maintain that concern for one's own good (self-interest) is sometimes morally outweighed by concern for the good of others (altruism), sometimes even to the point of *requiring* the sacrifice or restriction of one's own good for the good of others. Fortunately, Rand's critique of utilitarian and Kantian ethics does not depend on interpreting altruism as being radically opposed to self-interest. Her main argument can still be advanced against the moderate form of altruism actually endorsed by utilitarian and Kantian ethics.

We can see this by looking at (part of) a speech that is given in *The Fountainhead* by Howard Roark, who represents Rand's ideal of a self-interested man.[14] When he gives this speech at the end of the novel, Roark is on trial for dynamiting a building project that he had designed. He had secretly agreed to provide the architectural design for the project, without any monetary compensation, to the official architect of the project, Peter Keating, but only on the condition that his design not be altered in any way. Keating needed Roark's help because only Roark knew how to design the project so as to provide sufficient low-income housing within the budget constraints. As the project was being built, however, Keating succumbed to pressure to alter its design in ways that destroyed the aesthetic unity that Roark had given it. So as the project was nearing completion, Roark, aided by Dominique Francon, Rand's ideal of a self-interested woman in-the-making, blew the building up with dynamite. At his trial, which provides the climax to the novel, Roark offered the following defense for his action that secured for him an acquittal:

> It is said that I have destroyed the home of the destitute. It is forgotten that but for me the destitute could not have had this particular home. Those who were concerned with the poor had to come to me, who have never been concerned, in order to help the poor. It is believed that the poverty of the future tenants gave them a right to my work. That their need constituted a claim on my life. That it was my duty to contribute anything demanded of me. ... I came here to say that I do not recognize anyone's right to one minute of my life. Nor to any part of my energy. Nor to any achievement of mine. No matter who makes the claim, how large their number, or how great their need.[15]

Notice that although Roark does reject altruism in his speech, he can be understood to be rejecting the moderate form of altruism actually endorsed by Kantian and utilitarian ethics as well as the extreme form of altruism that Rand claims to be against. So it's preferable to make the real target of Rand's argument the moderate form of altruism that both utilitarian and Kantian ethics actually endorse.

THE NO-CONFLICT THESIS

Now one might think that a major problem with Rand's view is that it would give rise to fundamental moral conflicts when the self-interests of people conflict. In such cases, morality would require opposing actions that couldn't all be performed. Morality would thus cease to be an appropriate action-guide because it would no longer provide directives that all of us together could succeed in carrying out.

Rand's response to this problem is to deny the premise on which it is based, namely, that there are conflicts of self-interest between people. As Rand sees it, "there are no conflicts of interest among rational men."[16] To support her view, Rand invites us to consider the following case:

> Suppose two men [let's call them Abe and Alfie] apply for the same job. Only one of them can be hired. Isn't this an instance of conflict of interest, and isn't the benefit of one man achieved at the price of a sacrifice of the other?[17]

Rand argues that if Abe is offered the job because of his superior qualifications, it is false to say that the benefit Abe achieved is "at the price of a sacrifice" of Alfie. And Rand is clearly right about this. Under these circumstances, Alfie does not sacrifice anything. That would require that Alfie is deprived of something that he first legitimately possessed. Rather, he just loses out in this competition with Abe.

Still we might ask: Does Alfie's losing out in this competition conflict with Alfie's interest? Surely, this would not be the case if there happens to be another equally attractive job that Alfie can get instead. But suppose no other equally attractive job exists for Alfie. Under these circumstances, it seems clear that Alfie's losing out in this competition does conflict with what is in his interest. So contrary to what Rand claims, there is an interpersonal conflict of interest in this case.

Unfortunately, Rand's response to such cases does not directly address the question of whether there is a conflict of interest. For example, in the speech that we quoted from earlier, she has Roark say:

> I do not recognize anyone's right to one minute of my life. Nor to any part of my energy. Nor to any achievement of mine. No matter who makes the claim, how large their number, or how great their need.[18]

Similarly, in *Atlas Shrugged*, John Galt, who, like Howard Roark, also represents Rand's ideal of a self-interested man, makes a comparable claim in a lengthy radio address at the end of that novel. He says:

> [L]earn to treat as the mark of a cannibal any man's demand for your help. To demand it is to claim that your life is his property—and loathsome as such a claim might be, there's something still more loathsome: your agreement.[19]

However, in neither Roark's speech nor Galt's radio address is Rand addressing the question of interpersonal conflicts of interest. Rather, she is denying that people's unmet basic needs, in themselves, impose an obligation on others to help satisfy them. Yet irrespective of whether there is such an obligation, using, for example, Jeto's surplus to meet Janet's basic needs still does conflict with using that same surplus to secure luxuries for Jeto. What is best for Janet's interests, therefore, clearly conflicts with what is best for Jeto's interests. Surely, this is an interpersonal conflict of interest if there ever was one.

CONFLICTS OF SELF-INTEREST IN RAND'S NOVELS

A further problem confronting Rand's view that there are no rational conflicts of interest is the conflict of interest that exists between the characters in her novels, particularly *The Fountainhead*. In *The Fountainhead*, many characters come into conflict with Rand's main protagonist, Roark. In some cases, however, it can be argued that the conflicts are not rational ones. For example, Peter Keating, a fellow architect who functions as a foil to Roark in the novel, is in conflict with Roark at a number of key junctures throughout the novel. Still, it can be argued that when Keating acts against Roark's interests, he is also acting against his own, and so his conflicts with Roark are not rational ones. Given what we are told about Keating, it is surely possible to imagine him pursuing another life history that would better serve his own interests while not putting him in conflict with Roark.

Nevertheless, no such alternative life history is possible for Ellsworth Toohey, the main antagonist to Roark in the novel. In his role as art critic for Wynand's newspaper, the *Banner*, Toohey is opposed to Roark from the start and his opposition never abates, but rather constitutes the central conflict of the novel. At first, when Roark's work is less known, Toohey attempts to retard the development of Roark's career by not mentioning his work in his column in the *Banner*. Later, when Roark's work begins to attract some attention, Toohey criticizes Roark's work in his column whenever he has the opportunity to do so. Toohey also manipulates Keating to oppose Roark's career. He even arranges for a wealthy entrepreneur Hopton Stoddard to commission Roark to design an important building so that he can later manipulate Stoddard to bring a lawsuit against Roark for malpractice. The bad publicity that Roark receives from losing that lawsuit makes it very difficult for him to find new work. However, as Roark's career begins to revive due to the interest of a few people who still appreciate his talent, Toohey's public opposition to Roark returns even stronger than before, continuing to the very end of the novel. Even Roark's climactic acquittal in his second trial does not represent a complete defeat for Toohey, who, after the *Banner* shuts down, easily acquires a good position at another newspaper.

Rand also has Toohey explain why he is opposed to creative people like Roark. It is because they challenge his way of acquiring power over other people. Toohey's approach is to convince people that their talents are really mediocre, and that they should, therefore, live in accord with mediocre standards under his leadership or the leadership of people like him. Roark's talent for independent creative excellence stands directly opposed to Toohey's way of acquiring power over people. Toohey knows he lacks talent like Roark's for independent creative excellence, yet he is also quite successful at what he does—manipulating people and gaining power of over them—something he clearly enjoys doing. More importantly, given his talents, it is not possible to construct an alternative life history for him—one that would better serve his interests without still putting him into conflict with people like Roark. At the end of the novel, like many a comic-book villain, Toohey is ready and waiting to ride out again to do battle with Roark or with some other embodiment of Rand's ideally self-interested person.

THE NO-DUTY THESIS

Nevertheless, even granting that there are rational conflicts of interest both in the real world and in Rand's novels, they still may not present a serious challenge to Rand's Aristotelian ethics. What concerns Rand most is to deny we have a duty to help the poor when we are rich or talented. So, she could allow that there are conflicts of interest between the poor and the rich or talented without giving up her main thesis.

Still, what about her main thesis? Is there not a duty to help the poor in such situations? Rand considers and rejects the possibility of such a duty arising in what she calls emergencies. For Rand, an emergency is "an unchosen, unexpected event, limited in time, that creates conditions under which human survival is impossible, such as a flood or earthquake."[20] For such emergencies, Rand claims

> ... any help [we] give (to others) is an exception, not a rule, an act of generosity, not a moral duty, that it is marginal and incident— as disasters are marginal and incidental in the course of human existence.[21]

Now one could question whether the acts of generosity that Rand permits here are not grounded in the same altruism that she rejects. Nevertheless, it is more important to question Rand's rejection of a duty to help the poor in such situations.

Consider: If there is no duty to help in such situations, then the rich and talented would be within their rights to refuse to help and the poor would have no moral recourse in the face of such a refusal. At the extreme, this would mean that the poor would be required to sit back and starve to death while the rich and talented were allowed to enjoy the benefit of their luxuries. But surely this would be an unreasonable requirement to impose on the poor, one that would violate that fundamental principle of morality (as discussed before) namely, an expanded "Ought" implies "Can" principle. According to this principle, morality cannot impose unreasonable demands on people. In the extreme case, requiring the poor to sit back and starve to death would clearly be an unreasonable demand, whereas requiring the rich and talented to forgo meeting some of their luxury needs would clearly not be an unreasonable demand.

Alternatively, we could use an expanded "Ought" implies "Can" principle to weigh the liberty of the poor against the liberty of the rich, as we did in our discussion of the libertarian interpretation of Kantian ethics. Either way the principle would support a duty to help the poor when their basic needs would not otherwise be met, or as Rand puts, when their survival as rational human beings through their whole lifespan is threatened.[22]

Rand, therefore, fails to establish that the only fundamental virtue that Aristotelian ethics needs is that of selfishness. As we have shown, Aristotelian ethics also needs the virtue of altruism sufficient to support a duty to help the poor when they are in need. Not surprisingly, the altruism required here will resemble the moderate form of altruism that is supported by both Kantian and utilitarian ethics.

THE IMPORTANCE OF REJECTING THE NO-CONFLICT THESIS

With respect to Rand's Aristotelian ethics, it is worth noting how important it is to show that her no-conflict thesis (there are no conflicts of interest among rational people) is false. If her no-conflict thesis were true, then two other more important theses of Rand—(1) her no-duty thesis (there is no duty to help those in need) and (2) her reject-altruism thesis (altruism should be rejected)—would follow straightforwardly from that thesis.

Consider: If Rand's no-conflict thesis were true, then there would be no conflict of interest between people. So what is in the interest of the rich and talented would not conflict with what is in the interest of the poor. So, there would be no point to requiring the rich and the talented to sacrifice their interests to help the poor because no such sacrifice would be needed. Accordingly, there would be no grounds for a duty to help the poor rather than benefit oneself because no such help would be needed. That should suffice to establish Rand's no-duty thesis.

Similarly, consider: If Rand's no-conflict thesis were true, people's interests would never conflict. So altruistic self-sacrifice would be pointless. People's interests could always be fully advanced without anyone sacrificing his or her interests. Of course, people could still sacrifice their interests for sake of the interests of others, but there would always be alternative ways that others could have benefited just as much without any such altruistic self-sacrifice. Given the pointlessness of self-sacrifice, no rational person would want to engage in such sacrifice, and no rational person would want to be the beneficiary of it. Altruism would be just a fool's game that no one should want to play and everyone should want to reject.

However, once we recognize that Rand's no-conflict thesis is false, we cannot use the thesis to establish either Rand's no-duty thesis or her reject-altruism thesis. We are then led to recognize a duty to help the poor when they are in need, and altruism also emerges as a respectable virtue to be weighed against the virtue of selfishness in a morally defensible Aristotelian ethics.

Not surprisingly, Rand's Aristotelian ethics is not the only version of Aristotelian ethics that has attempted to use a no-conflict thesis to support its conclusions. Some versions of Aristotelian ethics understand people's moral interests to be common interests that we all share and further maintain that these common interests do not conflict with our individual self-interest, or at least not when that interest is rational. Since on such views, our common interests are just self-interests that we happen to share with others, these versions of Aristotelian ethics are, in effect, endorsing the no-conflict thesis.[23] Unfortunately, all such versions of Aristotelian ethics run into problems analogous to those faced by Rand's attempt to employ the no-conflict thesis in her Aristotelian ethics.

Conclusion

Aristotelian ethics, as we have seen, regards ethics as a way of being rather than as a way of doing. This puts the focus on a virtuous life that is assumed to be required for happiness. Virtue is further characterized as a mean between two vices, one of excess and the other of defect. While Aristotle himself raises difficulties for his account of virtue, we have seen how it is possible to overcome those difficulties in a way that leads to greater compatibility with Kantian and utilitarian ethics. We have also seen that Aristotelian ethics, even the version defended by Rand which initially appears to be at odds with both utilitarian and Kantian ethics, can be seen to lead to similar practical requirements, especially once the no-conflict thesis that is endorsed by Rand and other Aristotelians is rejected and an expanded "Ought" implies "Can" principle is seen to play a significant role in determining the theory's practical requirements.

MySearchLab Connections

Watch. Listen. Explore. Read. MySearchLab is designed just for you. Each chapter features a customized study plan to help you learn key concepts and terms. Dynamic visual activities, videos, and readings found in the multimedia library will enhance your learning experience.

Here are a few questions and activities to help you understand this chapter:

1. How did Aristotle develop a list of virtues using his doctrine of the mean (p. 79)?

   Read "Aristotle," Multimedia Library, Web Resources, Internet Encyclopedia of Philosophy.

2. How did Ayn Rand further defend her no-conflict thesis (p. 85)?

   Read "Ayn Rand," Multimedia Library, Web Resources, Internet Encyclopedia of Philosophy.

Each chapter features a customized study plan to help you learn and review key concepts and terms.

Notes

1. Aristotle, *Nicomachean Ethics,* trans. David Ross, rev. J. L Ackrill and J. O. Urmson (New York: Oxford University Press, 1980), 1103a33.

2. Notice this is similar to the way we conceived of morality as compromise in Chapter 3.

3. Alasdair MacIntyre, *After Virtue*, rev. ed. (Notre Dame, IN: University of Notre Dame Press, 1984), Chapter 14.

4. Martha Nussbaum, "Non-Relative Virtues: An Aristotelian Approach," in *Ethics: The Big Questions*, 2nd ed., ed. James P. Sterba (Oxford: Blackwell, 2009), 349–370.

5. See Julia Annas, "Ancient Ethics and Modern Ethics" in *Ethics: The Big Questions*, 2nd ed., ed. James P. Sterba (Oxford: Blackwell, 2009), 419–434; Robert Adams, *A Theory of Virtue* (Oxford: Oxford University Press, 2006), Chapter 5.

6. Philippa Foot, *Virtues and Vices* (Berkeley: University of California Press, 1978), 8–18; Rosalind Hursthouse, *On Virtue Ethics* (Oxford: Oxford University Press, 1999); Marcia Baron, Philip Pettit, and Michael Slote, *Three Methods of Ethics* (Oxford: Blackwell Publishers, 1997), 3–91.

7. Walter Schaller, "Are Virtues No More than Dispositions to Obey Moral Rules?" *Philosophy* 20 (July 1990): 195–207.

8. Rosalind Hursthouse claims "that virtue ethics not only comes up with rules (. . . couched in terms that derived from the virtues and vices) but further, does not exclude the more familiar deontological rules." *On Virtue Ethics*, 39. Rules of the first sort would be of the less informative kind we considered. Those of the second sort would be of the more informative kind we considered.

9. Rosalind Hursthouse, "Normative Virtue Ethics," in *Ethics: The Big Questions*, 2nd ed., ed. James P. Sterba (Oxford: Blackwell, 2009), 389–399.

10. Aristotle, *Nicomachean Ethics,* 2203a-b.

11. For an argument that does lead to this conclusion, see Russ Shafer-Landau, *The Fundamentals of Ethics*, 2nd edition (New York: Oxford University Press, 2012), 268–270.

12. Ayn Rand, *The Virtue of Selfishness* (New York: The New American Library, 1964), viii.

13. Ibid., 30.

14. Rand still retains gender roles within her self-interested ideal. See Ayn Rand, "About a Woman President," in *The Voice of Reason,* ed. Leonard Peikoff and Peter Schwartz (New York: New American Library, 1988), 267–270.

15. Ayn Rand, *The Fountainhead* (New York: Bobbs-Merrill, 1943), 684.

16. Rand, *The Virtue of Selfishness*, 57.

17. Ibid.

18. Rand, *The Fountainhead*, 684.

19. Ayn Rand, *Atlas Shrugged* (New York: Random House, 1957), 984.

20. Rand, *The Virtue of Selfishness*, 54.

21. Ibid., 56.

22. Ibid., 26.

23. See, for example, Alasdair MacIntyre, *Dependent Rational Animals* (La Salle, IL: Open Court, 1999), 160.

Taking-Stock Interlude

In the Introduction, we cited the example of conditions on American Indian reservations in the United States, particularly the conditions on Pine Ridge Reservation in South Dakota, where the poverty rate is nearly 500 percent, the teenage suicide rate 400 percent and the infant mortality rate 500 percent higher than the national average, and the average life expectancy is 50 years.[1] Now we are in a position to ask whether utilitarian ethics, Kantian ethics, and Aristotelian ethics, given their most morally defensible formulations, would make different practical recommendations about what is the appropriate moral response to the conditions on these reservations.

According to utilitarian ethics, we are required to always choose whatever action or social policy would have the best consequences for everyone concerned. Yet we noted that this requirement to maximize utility is best interpreted as internally constrained by an expanded "Ought" implies "Can" principle that rejects any imposition that it would be unreasonable to require those affected to abide by.

So interpreted, it would appear to follow from utilitarian ethics that we ought to provide American Indians living on these reservations with the resources they would need for a decent life because that would presumably maximize utility overall, but whether we could be forced to do so would clearly depend on whether such an imposition would be judged as reasonable according to an expanded "Ought" implies "Can" principle.

Similarly for Kantian ethics, it would seem that a maxim to help others in need, like the American Indians living on these reservations in the United States, would pass Kant's Categorical Imperative test, allowing for some morally appropriate exceptions. But then to determine whether this requirement should be backed up with coercion would, just as in the case of utilitarian ethics, depend on whether that enforcement would be judged as reasonable by an expanded "Ought" implies "Can" principle.

Finally, for Aristotelian ethics, moral requirements are specified in terms of the virtuous life, where that is further specified by what a person at a particular stage of development should do next in order to become more virtuous. From this perspective, it would seem that we would be required to help those who are in need, like the American Indians living on certain reservations in the United States. However, in order to determine whether this requirement should be backed up with coercion would, just as with utilitarian ethics and Kantian ethics, depend on whether such an imposition would be judged as reasonable by an expanded "Ought" implies "Can" principle.

On this account, there is little reason to think that utilitarian ethics, Kantian ethics, and Aristotelian ethics, when given their most morally defensible interpretations, would not favor the very same practical requirements. So what we have here are *alternative approaches*—utilitarian ethics, Kantian ethics, and Aristotelian ethics approach moral issues in somewhat different ways—*combined with practical consensus*—because, given their most morally defensible interpretations, these three approaches favor similar practical requirements.

Note

1. Stephanie M. Schwartz, "The Arrogance of Ignorance: Hidden Away, Out of Sight and Out of Mind," *Link Center Foundation* (2006), http://www.linkcenterfoundation.org/id24.html; David Stannard, *American Holocaust* (New York: Oxford University Press, 1993), 106, 256–7. More recent data suggest that poverty rates are even higher on the Pine Ridge Reservation.

CHAPTER 7

The Challenge of Environmentalism

The failure of traditional ethics to sufficiently take into account the interests of nonhuman living beings is what gives rise to the challenge of environmentalism that traditional ethics is biased in favor of humans. Recent interest in this challenge to traditional ethics dates from the publication of Peter Singer's article, "Animal Liberation," in the *New York Review of Books* in 1973, followed by the publication two years later of his book of the same title.[1] Singer focused attention on two of the most serious forms of animal exploitation: factory farming and animal experimentation.

In factory farming, millions of animals are raised in such a way that their short lives are dominated by pain and suffering. Veal calves are put in narrow stalls and tethered with a chain so that they cannot turn around, lie down comfortably, or groom themselves. They are fed a totally liquid diet deprived of iron to promote rapid weight gain and to maintain anemia, and they are given no water because thirsty animals eat more than those who drink water. Animal experimentation is also a big business, involving about 200 million animals a year worldwide.[2] A large percentage of these animals are used in commercial toxicity tests, such as the rabbit-blinding Draize eye test and the widely used and widely criticized LD50 toxicity test designed to find the lethal dose for 50 percent of a sample of animals.

SINGER'S UTILITARIAN ENVIRONMENTALISM

Singer argues for the liberation of animals by comparing the bias against animals, which he calls "speciesism," with biases against blacks and women. According to Singer, the grounds we have for opposing racism and sexism are also grounds for opposing speciesism because all forms of discrimination run counter to the principle of equal consideration which is the central principle of utilitarian ethics. According to Singer, racists violate this principle by unjustifiably giving greater weight to the interests of members of their own race in cases of conflict; sexists violate this principle by unjustifiably giving greater weight to the interests of members of their own sex in cases of conflict; and speciesists violate this principle by unjustifiably giving greater weight to the interests of members of their own species in cases of conflict.

Animals have interests, Singer maintains, because they have a capacity for suffering and enjoyment. According to the principle of equal consideration, there is no justification for regarding the pain animals feel as less important than the same amount of pain (or pleasure) humans feel. As for the practical requirements of this view, Singer contends that we cannot go astray if we give the same respect to the lives of animals that we give to the lives of humans at a similar mental level. In the end, Singer thinks, this will require us to make radical changes in our diet; the farming methods we use; experimental procedures in many fields of science; our approach to wildlife and to hunting; the trapping and wearing of furs; and areas of entertainment like circuses, rodeos, and zoos.

REGAN'S KANTIAN ENVIRONMENTALISM

Around the same time that Singer was developing his utilitarian environmentalism on behalf of animal liberation, Tom Regan was proposing a Kantian environmentalism.[3] According to Regan, what is fundamentally wrong with our treatment of nonhuman animals is that it implies that they are simply resources for our use. Regan argues that the correct grounding for our duties to animals and their rights against us is their inherent value, which they possess, equally with ourselves as experiencing subjects of life. Because animals, who are experiencing subjects of life, are entitled to equal respect, Regan argues that we should totally abolish the use of animals in science, end commercial animal agriculture, and eliminate both commercial and sport hunting and trapping. To those who might concede that animals have inherent value but to a lesser degree than humans, Regan argues that this view would be defensible only if similarly deficient humans were also seen as having less inherent value—a stance Regan feels his opponents are not willing to take.

A serious problem with both Singer's and Regan's views, however, is that they both still appear to be biased against certain forms of life. In the case of Singer's view, it is not clear why only sentient beings count and not all living beings. Singer maintains that only sentient beings have interests in the sense that what we do matters to them, but why should this be grounds for excluding nonsentient living beings from moral consideration, given that although they are nonsentient, they still have a good of their own? In the case of Regan's view, it is not clear why only experiencing subjects of life have inherent value and not all subjects of life. Regan recognizes that nonexperiencing subjects of life have a good of their own, but he does not explain why this does not suffice for them to count morally. This particular challenge to both Singer's and Regan's views is taken up by biocentrists, such as Paul Taylor, who defend an alternative view that morally takes into account the interests of all individual living beings.[4]

BIOCENTRISM

To defend their view, biocentrists need a really good argument that nonhuman living beings have moral status. As we have seen in Chapter 4, a really good argument must not beg the question. So what we need is a nonquestion-begging argument that nonhuman living beings have moral status, which is to say that they should count morally. Is there such an argument?

Now right off, we might think that we have nonquestion-begging grounds for taking only the interests of humans into account, namely, the possession by human beings of the distinctive trait of rationality. But while human beings clearly do have this distinctive trait, members of nonhuman species also have distinctive traits that humans lack, like the homing ability of pigeons, the speed of the cheetah, and the ruminative ability of sheep and cattle. Nor will it do to claim that the distinctive trait that humans possess is more valuable than the distinctive traits that members of other species possess because there is no nonquestion-begging standpoint from which to justify that claim. From a human standpoint, rationality is more valuable than any of the distinctive traits found in nonhuman species, since, as humans, we would not be better off if we were to trade in that trait for the distinctive traits found in nonhuman species. Yet the same holds true of nonhuman species. Generally, pigeons, cheetahs, sheep, and cattle would not be better off if they were to trade in their distinctive traits for the distinctive traits of other species.

Of course, the members of some species might be better off if they could retain the distinctive traits of their species while acquiring one or another of the distinctive traits possessed by some other species. For example, we humans might be better off if we could retain our distinctive traits while acquiring the ruminative ability of sheep and cattle. That would increase the range of things we could eat. But many of the distinctive traits of species cannot be even imaginatively added to the members of other species without substantially altering the original species. For example, in order for the cheetah to acquire the distinctive traits possessed by humans, presumably it would have to be so transformed that its paws became something like hands to accommodate its humanlike mental capabilities, thereby losing its distinctive speed, and ceasing to be a cheetah. So possessing distinctively human traits would not be good for the cheetah. And with the possible exception of our nearest evolutionary relatives, the same holds true for the members of other species: They would not be better off having distinctively human traits. Only in fairy tales and in the world of Disney can the members of nonhuman species enjoy a full array of distinctively human traits. So there would appear to be no nonquestion-begging perspective from which to judge that distinctively human traits are more valuable than the distinctive traits possessed by other species, and so we have no nonquestion-begging grounds for denying that nonhuman species have moral status.

It is true, of course, that we humans through the use of our technology have made ourselves more powerful than other species, but as we know in human ethics, being powerful and being morally right are not the same thing.[5] Nor in human ethics is being powerful a requirement for having moral status.

It will also not do to point out that except for a few close evolutionary relatives, we humans are the only moral agents. Surely most sentient and all nonsentient nonhuman living beings lack this capacity. Yet all that follows from this is that we humans, as moral agents, can recognize who has moral status and act accordingly. It does not follow that we are the only ones who have that status. For something to have moral status simply requires that its interests should significantly constrain what moral agents can do to it in pursuit of their own interests. Beings that have moral status have a good of their own, and, on that account, they should not be treated as mere instruments for the welfare of others. Significantly, we have not come up with any nonquestion-begging grounds for not granting that all living beings have this status.

PRINCIPLES OF CONFLICT RESOLUTION

Nevertheless, even if we grant that all living beings have moral status, we can justify a preference for humans on grounds of preservation. Accordingly, we have

> *A Principle of Human Preservation:* Actions that are necessary for meeting one's basic needs or the basic needs of other human beings are permissible even when they require aggressing against the basic needs of individual animals and plants, or even of whole species or ecosystems.

Now needs, in general, if not satisfied, lead to lacks or deficiencies with respect to various standards. The basic needs of humans, if not satisfied, lead to lacks or deficiencies with respect to a standard of a decent life. The basic needs of animals and plants, if not satisfied, lead to lacks or deficiencies with respect to a standard of a healthy life. The basic needs of species and ecosystems, if not satisfied, lead to lacks or deficiencies with respect to a standard of a healthy living system. The means necessary for meeting the basic needs of humans can vary widely from society to society. By contrast, the means necessary for meeting the basic needs of particular species of animals and plants tend to be invariant.[6] Of course, while only some needs can be clearly classified as basic, and others clearly classified as nonbasic, there still are other needs that are more or less difficult to classify. Yet the fact that not every need can be clearly classified as either basic or nonbasic—as it similarly holds for a whole range of dichotomous concepts such as moral/immoral, legal/illegal, living/nonliving, human/nonhuman—should not immobilize us from acting at least with respect to clear cases.

In human ethics, there is no principle that is strictly analogous to this Principle of Human Preservation. There is a principle of self-preservation in human ethics that permits actions that are necessary for meeting one's own basic needs or the basic needs of other people, even if this requires failing to meet (through an act of omission) the basic needs of still other people. For example, we can use our resources to feed ourselves and our families, even if this necessitates failing to meet the basic needs of people in underdeveloped countries. But, in general, we don't have a principle that allows us to aggress against (through an act of commission) the basic needs of some people in order to meet our own basic needs or the basic needs of other people to whom we are committed or happen to care about. One place where we do permit aggressing against the basic needs of other people in order to meet our own basic needs or the basic needs of people to whom we are committed or happen to care about is our acceptance of the outcome of life and death struggles in lifeboat cases, where no one has an antecedent right to the available resources. For example, if you had to fight off others in order to secure the last place in a lifeboat for yourself or for a member of your family, we might say that you justifiably aggressed against the basic needs of those whom you fought to meet your own basic needs or the basic needs of the member of your family.

Now the Principle of Human Preservation does not permit aggressing against the basic needs of humans even if it is the only way to meet our own basic needs or the basic needs of other human beings. Rather this principle is directed at a different range of cases with respect to which we can meet our own basic needs and the basic needs of other humans simply by aggressing against the basic needs of nonhuman living beings. With respect to those cases, the Principle of Human Preservation permits actions that are necessary for meeting one's own basic needs or the basic needs of other human beings, even when they require aggressing against the basic needs of individual animals and plants, or even of whole species or ecosystems.

Of course, we could envision an even more permissive Principle of Human Preservation, one that would permit us to aggress against the basic needs of both humans and nonhumans to meet our own basic needs or the basic needs of other human beings. But while adopting such a principle, by permitting cannibalism, would clearly reduce the degree of predation of humans on other species, and so would be of some benefit to other species, it would clearly be counterproductive with respect to meeting basic human needs. This is because implicit nonaggression pacts based on a reasonable expectation of a comparable degree of altruistic forbearance from fellow humans have been enormously beneficial and were probably necessary for the survival of the human species. So it is difficult to see how humans could be justifiably required to forgo such benefits.

Moreover, beyond the prudential value of such implicit nonaggression pacts against fellow humans, there appears to be no morally defensible way to exclude some humans from their protection. This is because any exclusion would fail to satisfy an expanded "Ought" implies "Can" principle, given that it would impose a sacrifice on at least some humans that would be unreasonable to require them to accept.[7]

But are there no exceptions to the Principle of Human Preservation? Consider, for example, the following real-life case.[8] Thousands of Nepalese have cleared forests, cultivated crops, and raised cattle and buffalo on land surrounding the Royal Chitwan National Park in Nepal, but they have also made incursions into the park to meet their own basic needs. In so doing, they have threatened the rhino, the Bengal tiger, and other endangered species in the park. Assume that the basic needs of no other humans are at stake. For this case, then, would the would-be human guardians of these nonhuman endangered species be justified in preventing the Nepalese from meeting their basic needs in order to preserve these endangered species? It seems to me that before the basic needs of disadvantaged Nepalese could be sacrificed, the would-be human guardians of these endangered species first would be required to use whatever surplus was available to them and to other humans to meet the basic needs of the Nepalese whom they propose to restrict. Yet clearly it would be very difficult to have first used up all the surplus available to the whole human population for meeting basic human needs. Under present conditions, this requirement has certainly not been met. Moreover, insofar as rich people are unwilling to make the necessary transfers of resources so that poor people would not be led to prey on endangered species in order to survive, then the appropriate means of preserving endangered species should be to use force against such rich people rather than against poor people, like the Nepalese near Royal Chitwan National Park. So for all present purposes, the moral permissibility in the Principle of Human Preservation remains that of strong permissibility, which means that other humans are prohibited from interfering with the aggression against nonhumans that is permitted by the principle.[9]

Nevertheless, preference for humans can still go beyond bounds, and the bounds that are required are captured by the following:

> *A Principle of Disproportionality:* Actions that meet nonbasic or luxury needs of humans are prohibited when they aggress against the basic needs of individual animals and plants or even of whole species or ecosystems.

This principle is strictly analogous to the principle in human ethics that similarly prohibits meeting some people's nonbasic or luxury needs by aggressing against the basic needs of other people. Without a doubt, the adoption of such a principle with respect to nonhumans would significantly change the way we live our lives. Such a principle is required, however, if there is to be any substance to the claim that the members of all species have moral status. We can no more consistently claim that the members of all species count morally and yet aggress against the basic needs of animals or plants whenever this serves our own nonbasic or luxury needs than we can consistently claim that all humans have moral status and then aggress against the basic needs of other human beings whenever this serves our nonbasic or luxury needs. Consequently, if saying that species have moral status is to mean anything, it must be the case that the basic needs of the members of nonhuman species are protected against aggressive actions that serve to meet only the nonbasic needs of humans, as required by the Principle of Disproportionality. Another way to put the central claim here is to hold that having moral status rules out domination, where domination means aggressing against the basic needs of some for the sake of satisfying the nonbasic needs of others.

Nevertheless, in order to avoid imposing an unacceptable sacrifice on the members of our own species, we can also justify a preference for humans on grounds of defense. Thus, we have

> *A Principle of Human Defense:* Actions that defend oneself and other human beings against harmful aggression are permissible even when they necessitate killing or harming individual animals or plants, or even destroying whole species or ecosystems.

This Principle of Human Defense allows us to defend ourselves and other human beings from harmful aggression, first against our persons and the persons of other humans beings that we are committed to or happen to care about and second against our justifiably held property and the justifiably held property of other humans beings that we are committed to or happen to care about.

This principle is analogous to the principle of self-defense that applies in human ethics and permits actions in defense of oneself or other human beings against harmful human aggression. In the case of human aggression, however, it will sometimes be possible to effectively defend oneself and other human beings by first suffering the aggression and then securing adequate compensation later. Since in the case of nonhuman aggression by the members of other species with which we are familiar, this is unlikely to obtain when more harmful preventive actions such as killing a rabid dog or swatting a mosquito will be justified. There are simply more ways to effectively stop aggressive humans than there are to effectively stop the aggressive nonhumans with which we are familiar.

Lastly, we need one more principle to deal with violations of the previous three principles. Accordingly, we have

> *A Principle of Rectification:* Compensation and reparation are required when the other principles have been violated.

Obviously, this principle is somewhat vague, but for those who are willing to abide by the other three principles, it should be possible to remedy that vagueness in practice. Here too would-be human guardians of the interests of nonhumans could have a useful role figuring out what is appropriate compensation or reparation for violations of the Principle of Disproportionality, and, even more importantly, designing ways to get that compensation or reparation enacted.

INDIVIDUALISM AND HOLISM

It might be objected, however, that we have not yet taken into account the conflict between holists and individualists. According to holists, the good of a species, or the good of an ecosystem, or the good of the whole biotic community can trump the good of individual living things.[10] According to individualists, the good of each individual living thing must be respected.[11]

Now one might think that holists would require that we abandon the Principle of Human Preservation. Yet consider: Assuming that people's basic needs are at stake, how could it be morally objectionable for them to try to meet those needs, even if this were to harm nonhuman individuals, species, whole ecosystems, or even, to some degree, the whole biotic community? Of course, we can *ask* people in such conflict cases not to meet their basic needs in order to prevent harm to nonhuman individuals or species, ecosystems, or the whole biotic community. But if people's basic needs are at stake, it will be a very unusual case where we can reasonably demand that they make such a sacrifice.

We could demand, of course, that people do all that they reasonably can to keep such conflicts from arising in the first place, for, just as in human ethics, many severe conflicts of interest can be avoided simply by doing what is morally required early on. Nevertheless, when lives or basic needs are at stake, the individualist perspective seems generally incontrovertible. We cannot normally require people to be saints.

At the same time, when people's basic needs are not at stake, we would be justified in acting on holistic grounds to prevent serious harm to nonhuman individuals, species, ecosystems, or the whole biotic community. Obviously, it will be difficult to know when our interventions will have this effect, but when we can be reasonably sure that they will, such interventions (e.g., culling elk herds in wolf-free ranges or preserving the habitat of endangered species) would be morally permissible, and would even be morally required when the Principle of Rectification applies. This shows that it is possible to agree with individualists when the basic needs of human beings are at stake, and to agree with holists when they are not.

Yet this combination of individualism and holism appears to conflict with recognizing that all species have moral status by imposing greater sacrifices on the members of nonhuman species than it imposes on the members of the human species. Fortunately, appearances are deceiving here. Although the proposed resolution justifies imposing holism only when people's basic needs are not at stake, it does not justify imposing individualism at all. Rather it would simply permit individualism when people's basic needs are at stake. Of course, we could impose holism under all conditions. But given that this would, in effect, involve going to war against people who are simply striving to meet their own basic needs in the only way they can, as permitted by the Principle of Human Preservation, such impositions would generally not be justified. It would involve taking away the means of survival from people, even when these means are not required for one's own survival.

Nevertheless, this combination of individualism and holism may leave animal liberationists wondering about the further implications of this resolution for the treatment of animals. Obviously, a good deal of work has already been done on this topic. Initially, philosophers thought that humanism could be extended to include animal liberation and eventually environmental concern. Then Baird Callicott argued that animal liberation and environmental concern were as opposed to each other as they were to humanism.[12] The resulting conflict Callicott called "a triangular affair." Agreeing with Callicott, Mark Sagoff contended that any attempt to link together animal liberation and environmental concern would lead to "a bad marriage and a quick divorce."[13] Yet other philosophers, such as Mary Ann Warren, have tended to play down the opposition between animal liberation and environmental concern, and even Callicott now thinks he can bring the two back together again.[14] There are good reasons for thinking that such reconciliation is possible.

Right off, it would be good for the environment if people generally, especially people in the developed world, adopted a more vegetarian diet of the sort that animal liberationists are recommending. This is because a good portion of livestock production today consumes grains that could be more effectively used for direct human consumption. For example, 90 percent of the protein, 99 percent of the carbohydrate, and 100 percent of the fiber value of grain is wasted by cycling it through livestock, and currently 64 percent of the U.S. grain crop is fed to livestock.[15] So by adopting a more vegetarian diet, people generally, and especially people in the developed world, could significantly reduce the amount of farmland that has to be kept in production to feed the human population. This, in turn, could have beneficial effects on the whole biotic community by eliminating the amount of soil erosion and environmental pollutants that result from raising livestock. For example, it has been estimated that 85 percent of U.S. topsoil lost from cropland, pasture, range land, and forest land is directly associated with raising livestock.[16] So, in addition to preventing animal suffering, there are these additional reasons to favor a more vegetarian diet.

But even though a more vegetarian diet seems in order, it is not clear that the interests of farm animals would be well served if all of us became complete vegetarians. Sagoff assumes that in a completely vegetarian human world, people would continue to feed farm animals as before.[17] But it is not clear that we would have any obligation to do so. Moreover, in a completely vegetarian human world, we would probably need about half of the grain we now feed livestock to meet people's nutritional needs, particularly in underdeveloped countries. There simply would not be enough grain to go around. And then there would be the need to conserve cropland for future generations. So in a completely vegetarian human world, it seems likely that the population of farm animals would be decimated, relegating many of the farm animals that remain to zoos. But raising farm animals can be seen to be mutually beneficial for humans and the farm animals involved. Surely, it would benefit farm animals to be brought into existence, maintained under healthy conditions, and hence not in the numbers sustainable only with factory farms, but then killed relatively painlessly and eaten, rather than that they not be brought into existence or maintained at all.[18] So a completely vegetarian human world would not be in the interest of farm animals. Of course, no one would be morally required to bring farm animals into existence and maintain them in this manner. Morally, it would suffice just to maintain representative members of the various subspecies in zoos. Nevertheless, many will find it difficult to pass up an arrangement that is morally permissible and mutually beneficial for both humans and farm animals.

It also seems in the interest of wild species that no longer have their natural predators not to be at least therapeutically hunted by humans. Of course, where possible, it may be preferable to reintroduce natural predators. But this may not always be possible because of the unavoidable proximity of farm animals and human populations, and then if action is not taken to control the populations of wild species, disaster could result for the species and their environments. For example, ungulates (hooved mammals such as white-tailed and mule deer, elk, and bison) as well as elephants in the absence of predators regularly tend to exceed the carrying capacity of their environments.[19] So it may be in the interest of these wild species and their environments that humans intervene periodically to maintain a balance. Of course, there will be many natural environments where it is in the interest of the environment and the wild animals that inhabit it to be simply left alone. But here too animal liberation and environmental concern would not be in conflict. For these reasons, animal liberationists might seem to have little reason to object in this regard to the proposed combination of individualism and holism that is captured by these principles of conflict resolution.

AN OBJECTION FROM A SOMEWHAT ALIEN PERSPECTIVE

There remains, however, at least one serious objection to the biocentrism that we have been defending here. It might be argued that from a somewhat alien perspective, our view is not biocentric enough. Consider the following. Suppose our planet were invaded by an intelligent and very powerful species of aliens who can easily impose their will upon us. Suppose these aliens have studied the life history of our planet and they have come to understand how we have wreaked havoc on our planet, driving many species into extinction, and how we still threaten still many other species with extinction. In short, suppose these aliens discover that we are like a cancer on our biosphere.

Suppose further that these aliens are fully aware of the differences between us and the other species on the planet. Suppose they clearly recognize that we more closely resemble them in power and intelligence than any other species on the planet. Even so, suppose the aliens still choose to protect those very species we threaten. They begin by forcing us to use no more resources than we need for a decent life, and this significantly reduces the threat we pose to many endangered species. However, the aliens want to do more. In order to save more endangered species, they decide to exterminate a certain portion of our human population, reducing our numbers to those we had when we were more in balance with the rest of the biosphere.

Now if this were to happen, would we have moral grounds to object to these actions taken by the aliens? Of course, we could argue that it would be unreasonable for us to do more than restrict ourselves to the resources we need for a decent life, and so we are not morally required to do to ourselves what the aliens are doing to us. But these aliens need not be denying this. They may recognize that the extermination of a certain portion of the human population is not something that humans could reasonably require of one another. What they are claiming, as champions of endangered species, is just the right to impose a still greater restriction on humans, recognizing, at the same time, a comparable right of humans to resist that imposition as best they can. Of course, in the imagined case, any resistance by humans would be futile; the aliens are just too powerful.

In so acting, the aliens would have placed themselves outside the morality captured by our principles of conflict resolution. The moral permissibility to meet one's basic needs and to defend oneself guaranteed by the Principles of Human Preservation and Human Defense, respectively, imply that any would-be guardians of the interests of nonhuman earthly species are morally prohibited from interfering with humans who are taking the necessary actions to preserve and defend themselves, even when this requires that the humans aggress against the basic needs of nonhumans. In our imaginary tale, however, the aliens have rejected this moral prohibition, claiming instead that it is morally permissible for them to ally themselves with the interests of some of the endangered species on our planet. The aliens claim that we cannot morally blame them, or morally object to what they are doing. They say that they have a right to try to impose greater restrictions on our species, and that we have a right to resist. And they would be right. How could we object to the actions of these nonhuman species–loving aliens?

Likewise, we could not object if similar actions were undertaken by radical Earth Firsters who, so to speak, chose to "go native" and renounce, to some extent, their membership in the human community so as to be able to take stronger steps to protect endangered species. Of course, we might argue that there are other more effective ways for these Earth Firsters to protect endangered species, but if their actions proved to be the most effective at protecting endangered species, what could our objection be? Of course, we could oppose them if they go beyond what is morally required, as we could oppose the aliens on those same grounds, but, as in the case of the aliens, we don't seem to have any moral objection against what they are doing. What this would show is that while morality cannot impose requirements that would be unreasonable to accept (i.e., requirements that violate an expanded "Ought" implies "Can" principle), it can permit (as it does here) actions that it cannot impose, as in lifeboat cases.[20]

Even so, before these radical Earth Firsters could sacrifice the basic needs of fellow humans for the sake of endangered species, they would be first required to use whatever surplus was available to them and to other humans before they sacrifice the basic needs of fellow humans for the sake of endangered species. Yet clearly it would be very difficult to have first used up all the surplus available to the whole human population that could be used to preserve endangered species.[21] Under present conditions, this requirement has certainly not been met. So unlike our imaginary aliens, who we assumed were first able to force us to use no more resources than we needed for a decent life, before they started killing us to further reduce the threat we pose to endangered species, the efforts of radical Earth Firsters would probably never get beyond that first step. All of their efforts would be focused on trying to benefit endangered species by forcing humans to use no more resources than they need for a decent life. Unlike our imaginary aliens, real-life radical Earth Firsters would probably never be able to justifiably get to the second step of taking the lives of fellow humans to benefit endangered species.

Accordingly, even though we can envision the perspective of hypothetical aliens and radical Earth Firsters and recognize that it is a morally permissible stance to take, that still doesn't undercut the moral defensibility of the Principles of Human Preservation, Disproportionality, Human Defense, and

Rectification. These principles still capture the moral requirements we can reasonably require all human beings to accept. In fact, the first step of this somewhat alien perspective requires the enforcement of just those principles. It is only at the second step, hypothetically justified in the case of the aliens, and virtually never justifiably realized in the case of real-life radical Earth Firsters, that we envision a departure from these principles. Hence, the mere possibility of this somewhat alien moral perspective does not undercut the real-life moral defensibility of these principles of conflict resolution.

Of course, reflecting on how these principles are to be implemented, someone could ask: How do you distinguish basic from nonbasic needs? A person raising this question may not realize how widespread the use of this distinction is. While the distinction is surely important for global ethics, as our use of it attests, it is also used widely in moral, political, and environmental philosophy; it would really be impossible to do much philosophy in these areas, especially at the practical level, without a distinction between basic and nonbasic needs. Another way to respond to the question is by pointing out that the fact that not every need can be clearly classified as either basic or nonbasic—as similarly holds for a whole range of dichotomous concepts such as moral/immoral, legal/illegal, living/nonliving, human/nonhuman—should not immobilize us from acting at least with respect to clear cases. This puts our use of the distinction in a still broader context suggesting that if we cannot use the basic/nonbasic distinction in moral, political, and environmental philosophy, the widespread use of other dichotomous concepts is likewise threatened. It also suggests how our inability to clearly classify every conceivable need as basic or nonbasic should not keep us from using such a distinction at least with respect to clear cases.

There is also a further point to be made here. If we begin to respond to clear cases, for example, stop aggressing against the clear basic needs of some for the sake of clear luxury needs of others, we will be in an even better position to know what to do in the less clear cases. This is because sincerely attempting to live out one's practical moral commitments helps one to interpret them better, just as failing to live them out makes interpreting them all the more difficult. Consequently, it would appear that we have every reason to act on the principles of conflict resolution defended in this chapter, at least with respect to clear cases.

Conclusion

Traditional ethics has been challenged as being biased against nonhuman living beings. To best avoid that bias, it was argued in this chapter that traditional ethics should endorse a version of biocentrism. This view requires accepting the Principle of Human Defense, the Principle of Human Preservation, the Principle of Disproportionality, and the Principle of Rectification as the appropriate priority resolution principles for resolving conflicts between humans and nonhuman living beings.

MySearchLab Connections

Watch. Listen. Explore. Read. MySearchLab is designed just for you. Each chapter features a customized study plan to help you learn key concepts and terms. Dynamic visual activities, videos, and readings found in the multimedia library will enhance your learning experience.

Here are a few questions and activities to help you understand this chapter:

1. What are the historical origins of the environmental challenge to traditional ethics (p. 95)?

   📖 Read "Environmental Ethics," Multimedia Library, Web Resources, Stanford Encyclopedia of Philosophy.

2. What are some other arguments for and against Peter Singer's and Tom Regan's defenses of the moral status of nonhuman animals (pp. 95–96)?

   📖 Read "Animals and Ethics," Multimedia Library, Web Resources, Internet Encyclopedia of Philosophy.

Each chapter features a customized study plan to help you learn and review key concepts and terms.

Notes

1. Peter Singer, *Animal Liberation*, rev. ed. (New York: Avon Books, 1992).

2. Bernard Rollins, *Animal Rights and Human Morality*, 2nd ed. (New York: Prometheus Books, 1992), Chapter 3; Alex Fino, *Lethal Laws* (New York: Zed Books, 1997), Chapter 1; Andrew Knight, *The Costs and Benefits of Animal Experimentation* (2011).

3. Tom Regan, *The Case for Animal Rights* (Berkeley: University of California Press, 1983).

4. See Paul Taylor, *Respect for Nature* (Princeton, NJ: Princeton University Press, 1987). The particular form of biocentrism that I would want to defend would give moral status to species as well as all individual living beings. But I will ignore that complication here.

5. By human ethics, I simply mean those forms of ethics that assume, without argument, only human beings count morally.

6. For further discussion of basic needs, see James P. Sterba, *How to Make People Just* (Totowa, NJ: Rowman and Littlefield, 1988), 45ff.

7. For a discussion of the expanded "Ought" implies "Can" principle, see Chapter 4.

8. See Holmes Rolston III, "Enforcing Environmental Ethics: Civil Law and Natural Value," in *Social and Political Philosophy: Contemporary Perspectives*, ed. James P. Sterba (London: Routledge, 2001), 349–369.

9. In the nonideal world in which we live, the Nepalese and their human allies should press rich people to acquire the available surplus to meet the basic needs of the Nepalese until their own lives are threatened. At that point, regrettably, the Nepalese would be justified in preying on endangered species as the only way for them to survive.

10. Aldo Leopold's view is usually interpreted as holistic in this sense. Leopold wrote, "A thing is right when it tends to preserve the integrity, stability and beauty of the biotic community. It is wrong when it tends otherwise." See Aldo Leopold, *A Sand County Almanac* (Oxford: Oxford University Press, 1949) 262.

11. For a defender of this view, see Taylor, *Respect for Nature*.

12. Baird Callicott, "Animal Liberation: A Triangular Affair," *Environmental Ethics* 2 (1980): 311–28.

13. Mark Sagoff, "Animal Liberation and Environmental Ethics: Bad Marriage, Quick Divorce," *Osgood Hall Law Journal* 22 (1984): 297–307.

14. Mary Ann Warren, "The Rights of the Nonhuman World," in *Environmental Philosophy*, eds. Robert Elliot and Arran Gare (University Park: Penn State University Press, 1983), 109–34; Baird Callicott, *In Defense of the Land Ethic* (Albany: State University Press of New York, 1989), Chapter 3.

15. EarthSave Foundation, *Realities for the 90's* (Santa Cruz, CA: EarthSave Foundation, 1991), 4.

16. Ibid., 5. See also John Robbins, *Diet for a New America* (Tiburon, CA: HJ Kramer, 1998).

17. Sagoff, "Animal Liberation and Environmental Ethics: Bad Marriage, Quick Divorce," 301–5.

18. There is an analogous story to tell here about "domesticated" plants, but there is no analogous story to tell about "extra humans" who could be raised for food given that the knowledge these "extra humans" would have of their fate would most likely make their lives not worth living. But even assuming that this is not the case and that this particular justification for domestication is ruled out because of its implications for a similar use of humans, it still would be the case that domestication is justified in a sustainable agriculture to provide fertilizer for crops to meet basic human needs.

19. There are other species, such as mourning doves, cottontail rabbits, gray squirrels, and bobwhite and blue quail, that each year produce more young than their habitat can support through the winter. But they usually do not degrade their environment. With respect to such species, it might be argued that hunting is morally permissible. Nevertheless, unless such hunting is either therapeutic or required to meet basic human needs, it is difficult to see how it could be permissible.

20. The direct analogy is to a lifeboat case in which you try to secure a lifeboat for one person from someone else who has an equal claim to it.

21. This is what I argued presently holds with regard to the means for protecting endangered species in the Royal Chitwan National Park in Nepal.

CHAPTER 8

The Challenge of Feminism

T he failure of traditional ethics to sufficiently take into account the interests of women is what gives rise to the feminist challenge that traditional ethics is biased in favor of men. Recent interest in this challenge dates from the publication of Carol Gilligan's *In a Different Voice* in 1982.[1] In this chapter, it will be argued that this bias of traditional ethics is manifested by the practical inadequacy of (1) its theories of justice and (2) its ideals of a morally good person. It will also be suggested in each case how this bias can be corrected.[2]

GILLIGAN'S CHALLENGE

In her influential work, *In a Different Voice*, Gilligan argues against the then prevailing view that women's moral development tends to lag behind that of men's. According to Gilligan, men and women do tend to make different moral judgments, but there is no basis for claiming that the moral judgments of men are better than those of women. All we can justifiably say is that they are different.

Gilligan goes on to contrast a care perspective favored by women with a justice perspective favored by men. According to Gilligan, these two perspectives are analogous to the alternative ways we tend to organize ambiguous perceptual patterns, for example, seeing a figure first as a square then as a diamond depending upon its relationship to the surrounding frame. More specifically, Gilligan claims:

> From a justice perspective, the self as moral agent stands as the figure against a ground of social relationships, judging the conflicting claims of self and others against a standard of equality or equal respect (the Categorical Imperative, the Golden Rule). From a care perspective, the relationship becomes the figure, defining self and others. Within the context of relationship, the self as a moral agent perceives and responds to the perception of need. The shift in moral perspective is manifest by a change in the moral question from "What is just?" to "How to respond?"[3]

Using these perspectives as classificatory tools, Gilligan reports that 69 percent of her sample raised considerations of both justice and care, while 67 percent focused their attention on one set of concerns (with focus defined as 75 percent or more of the considerations raised pertaining either to justice or to care). Significantly, with one exception, all of the men who focused, focused on justice. The women were divided, with roughly one-third focusing on care and one-third on justice.[4] The conclusion that Gilligan draws from this research is that the care perspective is an equally valid moral perspective that has tended to be disregarded in moral theory and psychological research alike because of male bias.

Critics, however, have questioned to what degree Gilligan has succeeded in specifying two contrasting perspectives.[5] At one point, Gilligan characterizes the justice perspective by the injunction "do not act unfairly toward others" and the care perspective by the injunction "do not turn away from someone in need."[6] But these two injunctions are inextricably linked in some conceptions of justice. For example, in a welfare liberal conception of justice with its ideal of fairness, to treat people fairly is to respond to their needs.

Sometimes Gilligan defends her distinction between a justice perspective and a care perspective by characterizing a justice perspective in an even more restrictive way as simply requiring a right of noninterference and a corresponding duty of others not to interfere.[7] Similarly, the editors of a collection of essays inspired by Gilligan's work contend that in a justice perspective, "People are surely entitled to noninterference; they may not be entitled to aid."[8] But this is to identify a justice perspective with a libertarian view that purports to reject rights to welfare and equal opportunity. Thus, this characterization of a justice perspective again fails to countenance other conceptions of justice, such as a welfare liberal conception of justice or a socialist conception of justice, whose requirements clearly go beyond a right to noninterference.

Now it may be objected that while some justice perspectives might be shown to accord with the requirements of a care perspective, they cannot always do so, and, in at least some cases, where the two perspectives are in conflict, the care perspective can be seen to have priority over the justice perspective.

Virginia Held offers us an example of what she takes to be just such a case in which care has priority over justice.[9] A father of a young child is also a teacher with a special skill in helping troubled young children succeed academically. If this father devotes most of his time to helping troubled young children, and lets his wife and others care for his own child, he will accomplish a lot of good. Even if the father takes into account the amount of good he can accomplish by spending more time with his own child, the good he will accomplish by devoting more time to helping troubled young children succeed academically is far greater. Nevertheless, Held thinks that this is a case where the care perspective, which requires that the father spend more time with his child, has priority over the justice perspective, which requires that he spend more time helping troubled young children succeed academically.

Yet even supposing Held was right about the particular moral requirements in this case, it is not clear that this is a case where care has priority over justice. As Claudia Card has pointed out, it is possible to view the father's requirement to spend more time with his child as a requirement of (particular) justice.[10] Imagine that the child deserves more attention from his father, and that (particular) justice requires the father to give the child what he or she deserves. So construed, this would be a case where a requirement of (particular) justice has priority over the requirement of (universal) justice to help others in need.[11] Again, what this example illustrates is how difficult it is to distinguish between a justice perspective and a care perspective.

But if we can't distinguish in theory between a justice perspective and a care perspective, it will be impossible for researchers to use this distinction in practice to characterize people as focusing on one or the other perspective. Of course, people will tend to use the language of justice and rights with the frequencies Gilligan observes, but we will have to look behind this usage to see what people are claiming when they use or don't use this language. If there is no viable theoretical distinction between a justice perspective and a care perspective, people frequently will be found to express care and concern for the needs of others by using the language of justice and rights as well as by using the language of care.

THE PRACTICAL INADEQUACY OF TRADITIONAL THEORIES OF JUSTICE

Nevertheless, even if we cannot draw a viable theoretical distinction between a justice perspective and a care perspective because at least some conceptions of justice are quite capable of expressing care and concern for the needs of others, it is still possible to raise a feminist challenge to traditional ethics in this regard at the practical level. This is because even theoretically adequate conceptions of justice tend to be applied in practice in ways that do not properly take into account the interests of women.

Take, for example, John Rawls's theory of justice. Working within the Kantian tradition, Rawls maintains, as we noted before, that principles of justice are those principles that persons behind an imaginary veil of ignorance would unanimously agree should be followed. This imaginary veil extends to most of the particular facts about oneself—anything that would bias one's choice or stand in the way of a unanimous agreement. It masks one's knowledge of one's social position, talents, sex, race, and religion, but not one's knowledge of such general information as would be contained in political, social, economic, and psychological theories. Persons in this original position, Rawls claims, would choose certain principles of justice because they assume, among other things, that they have the capacity for what Rawls calls "a sense of justice," that is, the capacity to abide by the principles of justice they have chosen.[12] In Rawls's theory, this assumption of a capacity for "a sense of justice" is further grounded in the assumption that persons in his original position have been raised in just families.[13] But while Rawls thus grounds his principles of justice in the possibility of just families, Rawls himself, until relatively recently (1997)—more than twenty-five years after he published his monumental *A Theory of Justice*—had published nothing about the nature of just families.

Belatedly, in an article devoted largely to another topic, Rawls does include a section titled "On the Family as Part of the Basic Structure," where he takes up the question of what implications his conception of justice has for family life.[14] Here Rawls argues that "wives have all the same basic rights, liberties and opportunities as their husbands."[15] Unfortunately, Rawls never goes on to spell out what it would be like for wives to have such rights, liberties, and opportunities both inside and outside family structures as their husbands. So we never get a clear picture from him of what just family structures would be like.[16] Moreover, this failure to provide an adequate account of the structure of just families creates the presumption that existing family structures may be morally acceptable when, as many feminists have argued, they are, in fact, biased against women.[17]

Consider the following. Today on average, women working full time in the United States earn only 78 cents for every dollar men earn. Put another way, a college-educated woman working full time over forty years earns $434,000 less than her male counterpart.[18] Moreover, if part-time workers are included in this comparison, the gap in the United States rises, with women earning only about half of what men earn.[19] As feminists see it, a significant part of this gap is due to discrimination.

Is It Discrimination or Is It Choice?

What feminists see as discrimination, however, others see as women's choices. If women were only to choose differently, it is claimed, they would earn as much as men.[20] But it will not do to attribute the pay gap to women's choices unless we can go on to show that men and women have the same opportunities for choice such that when they do in fact choose differently, we can attribute that difference to their choice and not to some significant difference in the opportunities they have. So the key question is: Do women in the United States have the same opportunity as men to have both a family and a career?

Now as men and women form families, they can theoretically combine a career and family life in different ways. Theoretically, it is possible for them to either equally share the parenting and the breadwinner roles or for one of them to take on the role of the primary parent while the other takes on the role of the primary breadwinner.

Now consider the second possibility, and ask yourself what would have to be the case in order for women to have an equal opportunity to be either a primary parent or a primary breadwinner? Isn't the answer that this could be possible only if men were, on average, just as willing to take on the role of either primary parent or primary breadwinner? If men are not equally willing to take on either of these roles, it would appear that women would not have an equal opportunity to choose between them. This is because there would not be enough men willing to form families in which they are the primary parents to provide women with the equal opportunity to choose between the two roles. So women's ability to choose between these two roles is limited by men's unwillingness to be the primary parent. So despite the fact that in recent years more men have been willing to embrace the role of primary parent, the general reluctance of men to do so has deprived women of an equal opportunity to choose between the two roles.

Now it might be objected that a similar case could be made on behalf of men. Couldn't it be claimed that it is women's unwillingness to take on the role of primary breadwinner that keeps men from having an equal opportunity to be either primary parent or primary breadwinner? But empirically this just does not seem to be the case. At least in modern times, women have moved into the workforce wherever, and to whatever extent, they have been given the opportunity to do so. In so doing, they have opened up considerable opportunity for men to take on a greater parenting role. And although men now do more parenting and housework than, say in the 1960s, married full-time career women still do about twice as much parenting and housework each week as their male partners.[21] Other studies in the United States show that men perceive doing an almost equal amount of housework—48 percent—as *unfair* to themselves. According to these studies, men see the division as *fair* to both parties when they are doing 36 percent of the housework, and they see the inequality as *unfair* only when their wives are doing over 70 percent of the work.[22]

Fortunately the advance of equality does not crucially depend on men's equal willingness to take on the role of primary parent. This is because having a partner who is equally willing to be either a primary parent or a primary breadwinner is not that great, even for those women who happen to find one. In effect, fully utilizing this option would just reverse the situation in traditional households where the mother is the primary parent and the father is the primary breadwinner.

Studies have shown, however, that this traditional arrangement is not preferable to one in which the tasks of parenting and breadwinning are more equally shared. Although it is theoretically possible for couples to be equitable when the roles of parenting and breadwinning are kept separate, when couples organize their family life into separate spheres, it is very difficult psychologically to separate the rhetoric about equality (where we say that we are equal in our separate roles) from reality (where we still regard the breadwinner role as having the greater importance). Almost all the research in the United States on couples with separate spheres of influence finds that each partner does not share equal power.[23] One study found that the partner who provides more income has more decision-making power, and the greater the difference in incomes, the more decision-making power the higher earning partner tends to have.[24] Accordingly, once we recognize that both traditional marriages and the flip-flop alternative to traditional marriage where the woman is primary breadwinner and the man the primary parent are problematic, we can come to appreciate the advantages of the second way that women and men can combine a career and family life, that is, by equally sharing the parenting and the breadwinner roles. Furthermore, there is considerable evidence that children benefit more from equal rearing from both parents.[25] So the option of having just one parent doing all the childrearing for any length of time is, other things being equal, not optimal.

Yet no matter how desirable this equal sharing option may be in theory, it cannot effectively be realized in practice unless there are the following institutional supports:

1. A maternity leave policy that provides employed mothers job security and publicly financed wage replacements around the time of childbirth or adoption.

2. An additional parental leave policy that provides both parents periods of paid leave during their children's earliest years.

3. Parents should also be entitled to some time off in order to attend to short-term and unpredictable needs that occur throughout their children's lives, such as routine illness, a disruption of childcare, a school-related emergency—without the fear of job loss or lost pay.

4. There should also be a policy that subsidizes the costs of childcare available to all families on a sliding scale that is calibrated according to family income, the number of children, and their ages.[26]

Instituting these options would go far beyond the U.S. Family and Medical Leave Act of 1993 which provides for an *unpaid* leave only at the time of childbirth, adoption, or serious family medical conditions, but not beyond programs currently in place in Western Europe.[27] Moreover, the use of state and federal government intervention and funding in the United States to support such equal sharing family programs can be justified, as it is throughout Western Europe, on the grounds that well-raised children are a public good that should be supported with public interventions and funding.[28]

With such institutional supports, the general expectation will be that both parents will be able to make acceptable progress in their careers or jobs while approximately equally sharing responsibility for the childcare and housekeeping duties, supplemented by a desirable level of day care. This would allow them to develop themselves in a career or job outside the home and serve the best interests of their children. It is the best way of achieving equal opportunity between women and men. It is the only alternative that is fair to both women and men.

Sometimes it is argued that men lack the necessary housekeeping or child-rearing skills owing to a deficient upbringing in which they were taught that housekeeping and childrearing are not appropriate activities for men to undertake.[29] We need, therefore, to try to correct these unfortunate misperceptions through such measures as required educational programs in our schools, including colleges and universities, publicly funded advertising analogous to the advertising directed against smoking, prohibiting gender-based advertising directed at children, making the granting of marriage licenses conditional upon the completion of a special educational program that addresses the issue of equal opportunity and fairness in family life. In addition, public support, including tax exempt status, should be denied to institutions and organizations, such as private schools and churches, that are not premised on equal opportunity for women and men.

It might be objected, however, that at least within family structures, we should not use a standard of equal opportunity or fairness but rather one of love and affection. But a standard of love and affection that requires unfairness and imposes unequal burdens simply because of one's sex is *not* an adequate standard of love and affection. Love and affection within families can and should go beyond fairness or equal opportunity, but they should not go against them. Where there is proper love and affection, one doesn't need to demand fairness and equal opportunity. Rather, these values are embraced as part of the way we have of showing proper love and affection for others. Thus, proper love and affection within the family would refuse to deny women equal opportunity on the basis of their sex.

We are thus led to the conclusion that when Rawls's Kantian conception of justice is correctly applied to the family, it requires certain specific family structures that secure equal opportunity for women and men.[30] Unfortunately, the failure of Rawls, and most defenders of his view, to draw this conclusion indicates how the practical application of his theory has, in fact, been biased in favor of men.

In this respect, however, contemporary defenders of utilitarian- or Aristotelian-based theories of justice have fared no better. In applying their theories, barring rare exceptions, they too have failed to recognize that their theories require certain specific family structures that secure equal opportunity for both men and women.[31] So while their theories of justice are also theoretically adequate to take women's interests into account, utilitarians and Aristotelians have standardly applied their theories in ways that are, in fact, biased in favor of men. While the failure has been at the practical, not the theoretical, level, this failure at the practical level has unfortunately been widespread.

The problem is particularly severe because there is still so much inequality between men and women in society, and because most major figures in the history of ethics, such as Aristotle and Kant, have defended inequality of this sort as natural and right.[32] Consequently, the failure of contemporary moral philosophers to address and condemn this inequality between men and women when setting out their theories of justice shows a failure to take women's interests sufficiently into account, and thus is biased against them.

THE PRACTICAL INADEQUACY OF THE TRADITIONAL IDEALS OF A MORALLY GOOD PERSON

In addition to the practical inadequacy of its theories of justice, traditional ethics has also failed to properly take women's interests into account when specifying its ideals of a morally good person.

In the Kantian ethics developed by John Rawls, for example, a morally good person is one whose actions conform to the principles that would be unanimously chosen by persons behind an imaginary veil of ignorance.[33] These principles specify the proper distribution of basic liberties, opportunities, and economic goods in society, and what rights and duties people have with respect to these social goods. While morally good persons will go beyond these principles to endorse particular comprehensive conceptions of the good, what they all have in common, according to Rawls, is that they would abide by the principles that would be chosen in his original position.

In utilitarian ethics, a morally good person is one whose actions maximize the net utility or satisfaction of everyone affected by them, compatible with not violating an expanded "Ought" implies "Can" principle. But normally in order for a person's action to maximize net utility, a person needs to follow certain rules and practices. Trying to directly determine with respect to each of our actions what would maximize net utility would not only require far more reflection than we are capable of, it would also be counterproductive. So in utilitarian ethics, a morally good person is one who generally follows the best rules and practices for maximizing utility in his or her society and only attempts to directly calculate the utility of the available options when those rules and practices come into conflict.

In Aristotelian ethics, a morally good person is one whose actions, for the most part, further his or her happiness, properly understood. For Aristotelians, one's happiness, properly understood, is further specified as acting in conformity with a set of virtues, the most important of which are prudence, justice, courage, and temperance, and what these virtues require is generally determined by the morally best practices of one's society.

Now while Kantian ethics, utilitarian ethics, and Aristotelian ethics all specify their ideals of a morally good person somewhat differently, from a feminist standpoint, the general problem with them all is that they specify their ideals so abstractly that they fail to deal with the question of whether we should conform to the distinctive gender roles that women and men are socialized into in our society. Thus, when we think stereotypically about men and women in our society, we still come up with lists of contrasting traits such as the following:

Men	**Women**
Dominant	*Submissive*, self-effacing
Independent	*Dependent*
Competitive	Cooperative
Aggressive, assertive	Nurturant, caring
Unemotional, stoic, detached	Emotional
Active, *violent*	*Passive*, nonviolent
Unconcerned with appearance	*Concerned with appearance (vain)*
Decisive	*Indecisive*
Seen as subject	Seen as object (of beauty or sexual attraction)
Sloppy	Neat
Sexually active	*Slut or nun*
Reasonable, rational, logical	Intuitive, *illogical*
Protective	In need of protection
Insensitive	Sensitive

If we assume that the traits in *italics* are obviously undesirable ones, then in addition to having quite different stereotypical traits associated with men and women in our society, we also have more undesirable traits on the women's list than on the men's.[34]

How should we think about such lists? Surely they reflect the gender roles and traits which boys and girls, men and women are socialized into in society. In the past, the desirable gender traits stereotypically associated with men were thought to characterize mental health.[35] More recently, these same traits have been used to describe the successful corporate executive.[36] Distinctive gender roles and traits have been used in these ways to favor men over women. Nevertheless, traditional ethics with its relatively abstract specification of its ideals of a morally good person has failed to take up the question of whether we should conform to those distinctive gender roles, thereby, through neglect, implicitly endorsing those same gender roles and traits. This has rendered the traditional ideals of a morally good person practically inadequate in a way that is biased against women.

Nor is traditional ethics without resources to deal with the question of gender roles in society. If we want to adequately take into account the interests of women, the appropriate answer to the question of whether we should maintain distinctive gender roles and traits in society is clear. It is that we need to replace these distinctive gender roles and traits with an ideal which makes all truly desirable traits that can be distributed in society equally open to both women and men. More accurately, we need to require that the traits that are truly desirable and distributable in society be equally open to both women and men or, in the case of virtues, equally expected of both women and men, other things being equal.

To distinguish traits of character that are virtues from those that are merely desirable, let us define the class of virtues as those desirable and distributable traits that can be reasonably expected of both women and men. Admittedly, this is a restrictive use of the term *virtue*. In normal usage, *virtue* is almost synonymous with *desirable trait*.[37] But there is good reason to focus on those desirable traits that can be justifiably inculcated in both women and men, and so for our purposes let us refer to this class of desirable traits as virtues.

So characterized, this ideal represents neither a revolt against so-called feminine virtues and traits nor their exaltation over so-called masculine virtues and traits.[38] This is because the ideal does not view women's liberation as simply the freeing of women from the confines of traditional roles, which makes it possible for them to develop in ways heretofore reserved for men. Nor does the ideal view women's liberation as simply the reevaluation and glorification of so-called feminine activities, like housekeeping or mothering or so-called feminine modes of thinking as reflected in an ethic of care. The first perspective ignores or devalues genuine virtues and desirable traits traditionally associated with women, while the second ignores or devalues genuine virtues and desirable traits traditionally associated with men. In contrast, this ideal seeks a broader-based ideal for both women and men that combines virtues and desirable traits traditionally associated with women with virtues and desirable traits traditionally associated with men. For this reason, we can call it the ideal of androgyny, a common ideal for both men (andro-) and women (-gyne).

This ideal of androgyny should be part of the practical specification of the ideals of a morally good person whether those ideals are Kantian, utilitarian, or Aristotelian. It should be seen as what persons behind an imaginary veil of ignorance, persons whose actions maximize the net utility or satisfaction of everyone affected by them, and persons seeking their own happiness properly understood would all endorse. Accordingly, only when traditional ethics includes the ideal of androgyny within the practical specification of its ideals of a morally good person, will it succeed in being practically adequate in a way that also avoids being biased against women.

It is also important to see that the ideal of androgyny which must be included in the practical specification of the ideals of a morally good person if traditional ethics is to succeed in being practically adequate is itself a specification of the ideal of equal opportunity. That is why, when we earlier applied the ideal of equal opportunity in order to determine just family structures as required by a practically adequate conception of justice, it ruled out the possibility of families where roles were assigned simply on the basis of gender. It is also why the various ways we have discussed of helping to create equal opportunity between women and men both inside and outside of family life, such as equal sharing of housekeeping and childrearing, paid maternity and parental leave, subsidized childcare, and prohibiting gender-based advertising directed at children, are also ways of helping to realize the ideal of androgyny. Here, an androgynous society and an equal opportunity society are one and the same.

Conclusion

In recent times, Carol Gilligan's work has given rise to the challenge that traditional ethics is biased against women. In this chapter, it has been argued that the bias of traditional ethics is manifested by the practical inadequacy of its theories of justice and its ideals of a morally good person. It has been further argued that traditional ethics can overcome this bias by applying its theories of justice and its ideals of a morally good person so as to determine just family structures and to implement an ideal of androgyny. This is what is required if traditional ethics is to meet the challenge of feminism and adequately take women's perspectives into account.

MySearchLab Connections

Watch. Listen. Explore. Read. MySearchLab is designed just for you. Each chapter features a customized study plan to help you learn key concepts and terms. Dynamic visual activities, videos, and readings found in the multimedia library will enhance your learning experience.

Here are a few questions and activities to help you understand this chapter:

1. What were the historical influences on Carol Gilligan's feminist challenge to traditional ethics (p. 109)?

   📖 Read "Feminist Ethics," Multimedia Library, Web Resources, Stanford Encyclopedia of Philosophy.

2. Is discrimination against women rooted in conventional gender roles that lead men and women to see the world differently (p. 115)?

   📖 Read "Feminist Standpoint Theory," Multimedia Library, Web Resources, Internet Encyclopedia of Philosophy.

Each chapter features a customized study plan to help you learn and review key concepts and terms.

Notes

1. Carol Gilligan, *In a Different Voice* (Cambridge: Harvard University Press, 1982).

2. It is commonly agreed upon among feminists that traditional ethics is biased against women and that this bias is manifested in the ways I suggest, but some feminists have argued that this bias is manifested in still others ways. For example, see Virginia Held, "Feminist Transformations of Moral Theory," in *Ethics: The Big Questions, ed. James P. Sterba* (Oxford: Blackwell, 1998), 331–45; Alison Jaggar, "Western Feminist Ethics," in *The Blackwell Guide to Ethics,* ed. Hugh LaFollette (Oxford: Blackwell, 2000), 348–74. Nevertheless, I think that all would agree that if the correctives proposed in this chapter were implemented, then virtually all forms of bias against women in traditional ethics would be corrected as well.

3. Carol Gilligan, "Moral Orientations and Moral Development," in *Women and Moral Theory,* ed. Eva Kittay and Diana Meyers (Totowa, NJ: Rowman and Littlefield, 1987), 23.

4. Ibid., 25.

5. Jean Grimshaw, *Philosophy and Feminist Thinking* (Minneapolis: University of Minnesota Press, 1986); James P. Sterba, *How to Make People Just* (Totowa, NJ: Rowman and Littlefield, 1988), 182–4; Will Kymlicka, *Contemporary Political Philosophy* (New York: Oxford, 1990), Chapter 7; Claudia Card, ed., *Feminist Ethics,*(Lawrence: University of Kansas Press, 1991); Eve Browning Cole and Susan Coultrap-McQuin, eds., *Exploration in Feminist Ethics* (Bloomington: Indiana University Press, 1992);

Virginia Held, ed., *Justice and Care* (Boulder, CO: Westview, 1995); Daryl Koehn, *Rethinking Feminist Ethics* (New York: Routledge, 1998).

6. Gilligan, "Moral Orientations and Moral Development," 20.

7. Ibid., 23; Gilligan, *In a Different Voice*, 100, 149.

8. Kittay and Meyers, *Women and Moral Theory*, 5.

9. Virginia Held, "Caring Relations and Principles of Justice," in *Controversies in Feminism*, ed. James P. Sterba (Lanham, MD: Rowman & Littlefield, 2000).

10. Claudia Card, "Particular Justice and General Care," in *Controversies in Feminism*, ed. James P. Sterba (Lanham, MD: Rowman and Littlefield, 2000).

11. Or maybe we should regard this as a case where one requirement of (particular) justice that the father give his child what he or she deserves has priority over another requirement of (particular) justice that he provide more of his students the help they need.

12. John Rawls, *A Theory of Justice* (Cambridge: Harvard University Press, 1971), 19, 491.

13. Ibid., 490.

14. John Rawls, "The Idea of Public Reason Revisited," *The University of Chicago Law Review* (1997): 787–94. Interestingly, Martha Nussbaum cites Rawls along with Susan Okin as a contemporary theorist of the family who has "asked how legal changes could promote respect for women's worth and autonomy, and ensure norms of fair equality of opportunity." But the only reference to Rawls other than to his *A Theory of Justice*, which just assumes that families are just, is to an unpublished manuscript. See Martha Nussbaum, *Cultivating Humanity* (Cambridge: Harvard University Press, 1997), 196, note #11.

15. Rawls, "The Idea of Public Reason Revisited," 789–90.

16. See Stephanie Coontz, *The Way We Never Were* (New York: Basic Books, 1992), 2–3, 16; Michael Wolff, *Where We Stand* (New York: Bantam Books, 1992), 23ff, 115; Deirdre English, "Through the Glass Ceiling," *Mother Jones* (November 1992): 49–54. The percentage of children living in poverty has increased still more as the result of the economic recession. See http://www.presstv.ir/detail/178645.html.

17. See, for example, the essays in *Feminism and Families*, ed. Hilde Lindemann Nelson (New York: Routledge, 1997).

18. Center for American Progress, *"Wage Gap by the Numbers," Center for American Progress*, January 6, 2009, http://www.americanprogress.org/issues/2009/01/wage_gap_numbers.html (accessed November 8, 2009).

19. Joan Williams, *Unbending Gender: Why Family and Work Conflict and What to Do About It* (New York: Oxford, 2000), 274.

20. Warren Farrell, *Why Men Earn More* (New York: AMACOM, 2005), Chapter 1.

21. Renge Jibu, "How American Men's Participation in Housework and Childcare Affects Wives's Careers," Center for the Education of Women, University of Michigan, July, 2007.

22. Virginia Valian, *Why So Slow?* (Cambridge: MIT Press, 1998), 40. What is even more surprising is that married women who work outside the home have similar cut-off points. They do not find the division as unfair to themselves until they are doing about 75 percent of the housework. When they are doing 66 percent of the work, they judge the division of housework as fair to both parties.

23. Pepper Schwartz, *Peer Marriage* (New York: Free Press, 1994), 4.

24. Ibid., 112.

25. Dorothy Dinnerstein, *The Mermaid and the Minotaur* (New York: Harper and Row, 1977); Nancy Chodorow, *Mothering: Psychoanalysis and the Sociology of Gender* (Berkeley: University of California Press, 1978); Vivian Gornick, "Here's News: Fathers Matter as Much as Mothers," *Village Voice*, October 13, 1975.

26. The elements of this feminist plan are supported by Joan Williams's *Unbending Gender*; Ann Crittenden, *The Price of Motherhood* (New York: Henry Holt, 2001); Janet Gornick and Marcia Meyers, *Families That Work* (New York: Russell Sage, 2003); Neil Gilbert, *The Transformation of the Welfare State* (New York: Oxford, 2002).

27. See Janet Gornick and Marcia Meyers, *Families That Work*, 117–128.

28. Ibid.

29. Lecturing in Leningrad in 1989, my partner, Janet Kourany, and I were told by two male university students that men were by nature incapable of cleaning toilets.

30. The problem raised here for a Rawls's welfare liberal interpretation of Kantian ethics is even more acute for a libertarian interpretation of the view. This is because a libertarian interpretation of Kantian ethics does not recognize that there is a need (following from its own ideal of liberty) to endorse something akin to a requirement of equal opportunity between men and women. See James P. Sterba, *Justice for Here and Now* (New York: Cambridge University Press, 1998), 60ff.

31. For one of these exceptions, working within the Aristotelian tradition, see the work of Martha Nussbaum, most recently, *Sex and Social Justice* (New York: Oxford University Press, 1998).

32. See the selections in James P. Sterba, *Ethics: Classical Western Texts in Feminist and Multicultural Perspectives* (New York: Oxford University Press, 1999).

33. Rawls, *A Theory of Justice*, 437.

34. It is also worth exploring how these specific traits are related to the more general traits of femininity and masculinity and whether the latter traits should be retained in a just society.

35. Beverly Walker, "Psychology and Feminism—If You Can't Beat Them, Join Them," in *Men's Studies Modified*, ed. Dale Spender (Oxford: Pergamon Press, 1981), 112–4.

36. Debra Renee Kaufman, "Professional Women: How Real Are the Recent Gains?" in *Feminist Philosophies*, 2nd ed., ed. Janet A. Kourany, James P. Sterba, and Rosemarie Tong (Upper Saddle River, NJ: Prentice-Hall, 1999), 189–202.

37. On this point, see Edmund Pincoffs, *Quandaries and Virtue* (Lawrence: University of Kansas, 1986), Chapter 5.

38. For a valuable discussion and critique of these two viewpoints, see Iris Young, "Humanism, Gynocentrism and Feminist Politics," *Women's Studies International Forum* 8 (1985): 173–83.

CHAPTER 9

The Challenge of Multiculturalism

The failure of traditional ethics to sufficiently take into account non-Western cultures especially with respect to the canon of what should be taught is what gives rise to the multiculturalist challenge that traditional ethics is biased in favor of Western culture. Interest in this challenge of multiculturalism to traditional ethics dates from a more general multicultural challenge to the educational canon that provoked a national debate in the United States in the late 1980s and early 1990s. This national debate focused on Stanford University's revision of its Western civilization course that introduced an *optional* eighth-track version of the course in which the required elements of the European canon remained, but were read along with works of Spanish American, American Indian, and African American authors. Even these minimal changes, however, were roundly attacked. For example, then Secretary of Education William Bennett paid a visit to Stanford to criticize the changes. George Will, in his national column, wrote that courses at Stanford should "affirm this fact: America is predominantly a product of the Western tradition and is predominantly good because that tradition is good."[1] William Buckley declared that "from Homer to the nineteenth century no great book has emerged from any non-European source."[2] In agreement with Buckley, Saul Bellow remarked, "When the Zulus have a Tolstoy, we will read him."[3] Such opposition to opening up the educational canon to non-Western sources is particularly striking when one recognizes that over 50 percent of the undergraduate students at Stanford, as well as at Berkeley and UCLA are nonwhite, as are over 30 percent of all U.S. undergraduate students. It is even more striking when one reflects that if current trends continue, a near majority of the U.S. population will be of minority origin by 2042.

Now the multicultural challenge to traditional ethics parallels this more general multicultural challenge to the educational canon. Its central claim is that if Western moral ideals are to be defensible, they must be able to survive a comparative evaluation with other moral ideals, including non-Western ones.[4] So it claims, there is no escaping an adequate representation of non-Western moral ideals in the canon of what should be taught.

It might be objected, however, that the justification of our moral ideals is not comparative, but rather grounded in a rationality that is required of each and every human being. Moreover, the argument offered at the end of Chapter 3 attempted to do just that—show that morality is required by rationality. Yet even assuming this attempt to show that morality is rationally required is successful, it would still not eliminate the need for a comparative evaluation of moral ideals. This is because the argument, if successful, succeeds only in showing that morality is rationally preferable to egoism or pure altruism. It does not establish which particular form of morality is preferable. To do that we still need a comparable evaluation of alternative moral ideals, and to avoid bias, that evaluation must also take into account non-Western as well as Western moral ideals.

Unfortunately, traditional ethics, by and large, has simply ignored the need for a comparative evaluation of this sort. It has rested content offering a comparative evaluation that is limited to Western moral ideals, mainly the utilitarian, Kantian, and Aristotelian perspectives discussed in Chapters 4–6. In this way, traditional ethics has shown itself to be biased against non-Western moral ideals and has thereby failed to provide an adequate justification of its own moral ideals.

Nevertheless, it might be objected that our rejection of moral relativism in Chapter 2 eliminates the need to examine the moral ideals found in other cultures, whether Western or non-Western, when trying to determine what is a defensible moral ideal for ourselves. But the multicultural challenge is quite different from the challenge of moral relativism that we have rejected. The multicultural challenge does not maintain that morality is relative to culture. Rather, it maintains that non-Western cultures may provide important insights into what is the most defensible moral ideal for ourselves, and if we fail to investigate non-Western cultures for such insights, we thereby jeopardize our chances of arriving at that ideal.

Consider a civil engineer, Sarah, who specializes in building bridges. Suppose Sarah has a chance to learn about how bridges are built in other countries with quite different cultures from her own. Other things being equal, shouldn't she be eager to learn about how bridges are built in those other countries? Might she not thereby be able to learn about some new building techniques that would actually improve her own way of building bridges? For a similar reason, we need to look to non-Western cultures for insights that could help us determine what the most defensible moral ideal for ourselves is. Only by engaging in such a comparative evaluation with non-Western cultures can traditional ethics avoid the multicultural challenge that it is biased against those cultures.

It is also important to reflect upon what sort of a comparative evaluation is needed here. The ethics we are looking for must be able to provide sufficient reasons accessible to all those to whom it applies so as to justify the enforcement of its requirements. This is because people cannot be justifiably forced to abide by ethical requirements if they cannot come to know, and so come to justifiably believe, that they should abide by those requirements. For an ethics is to be able to justify the enforcement of its requirements, therefore, there must be sufficient reasons accessible to all those to whom it applies to abide by those requirements. What this means is that the ethics must be secular rather than religious in character because only secular reasons are accessible to everyone; religious reasons are primarily accessible only to the members of the particular religious groups who hold them, and as such they cannot provide the justification that is needed to support the enforcement of the basic requirements of morality.

Accordingly, we are looking for an ethics that is secular in character and thus one that can provide sufficient reasons accessible to all those to whom it applies for abiding by the requirements it seeks to enforce. As such, it will be an ethics that is capable of justifying the enforcement of those requirements. So it will require a wide-ranging comparative evaluation of both Western and non-Western moral ideals. That is why the failure of traditional ethics to take into account non-Western moral ideals is so important. It is a challenge to the possibility of providing a defensible ethics for our time. That is why we must do what we can to meet this challenge to traditional ethics.

Now there are various ways that non-Western cultures can contribute to the fashioning of a defensible ethics for our times. In this chapter, we will consider three ways that they can do so. First, non-Western moral ideals can help to significantly correct and interpret our Western moral ideals themselves. Second, non-Western cultures can help us recognize important obligations that flow from our moral ideals that we either did not recognize or fully recognize before. Third, non-Western cultures can help us know how best to apply our own moral ideals, especially cross-culturally.

CORRECTING AND INTERPRETING TRADITIONAL ETHICS

Traditional ethics has focused on the debate between utilitarian, Kantian, and Aristotelian views. Yet however this debate is resolved, it still may be that traditional ethics is not demanding enough because it has not adequately faced the question of who is to count in ways that at least some non-Western moral perspectives have done. Here American Indian culture can be helpful.

Using American Indian Culture

In traditional ethics, it is assumed that only human beings have the moral status or count morally. By contrast, many, if not all, American Indian nations regard animals, plants, and assorted other natural things as having moral status and thus require that we show them respect. The type of respect required is illustrated by the following account of how a Sioux elder advised his son to hunt the four-legged animals of the forest.

> [S]hoot your four-legged brother in the hind area, slowing it down but not killing it. Then, take the four-legged's head in your hands, and look into his eyes. The eyes are where all the suffering is. Look into your brother's eyes and feel his pain. Then, take your knife and cut the four-legged under his chin, here, on his neck, so that he dies quickly. And as you do, ask your brother, the four-legged, for forgiveness for what you do. Offer also a prayer of thanks to your four-legged kin for offering his body to you just now, when you need food to eat and clothing to wear. And promise the four-legged that you will put yourself back into the earth when you die, to become the nourishment of the earth, and for the sister flowers, and for the

brother deer. It is appropriate that you should offer this blessing for the four-legged and, in due time, reciprocate in turn with your body in this way, as the four-legged gives life to you for your survival.[5]

Wooden Leg, a Cheyenne, provides a similar account:

The old Indian teaching was that it is wrong to tear loose from its place on the earth anything that may be growing there. It may be cut off, but it should not be uprooted. The trees and the grass have spirits. Whenever one of such growths may be destroyed by some good Indian, his act is done in sadness and with a prayer for forgiveness because of necessities. . . .[6]

Moreover, this respect for nonhuman nature shared by American Indians is based on a perceived shared identity with other living things. According to Luther Standing Bear, a Sioux chief,

We are the soil and the soil is us. We love the birds and beasts that grew with us on this soil. They drank the same water as we did and breathed the same air. We are all one in nature. Believing so, there was in our hearts a great peace and a welling kindness for all living growing things.[7]

Jorge Valadez has also pointed out that for the Mayans of Central America, nature is not something to be mastered and controlled for human purposes.[8] The Mayans saw themselves not as standing against nature but rather as an integral part of it. Arguably, it is this respect for nonhuman nature that has enabled people in non-Western cultures to live in their natural environment with greater harmony than we in Western culture are presently doing.

Is there, then, something that we in Western culture can learn from these non-Western cultures? At the very least, an appreciation for these cultures should lead us to consider whether we have legitimate grounds for failing to constrain our own interests for the sake of nonhuman nature. In Western culture, people tend to think of themselves as radically separate from and superior to nonhuman nature, so as to allow for domination over it. To justify this perspective, people in Western culture often appeal to the creation story in Genesis in which God tells humans to,

Be fruitful and multiply, and fill the earth and subdue it. Have dominion over the fish of the sea, the birds of the air, cattle, and all the animals that crawl on the earth.[9]

One interpretation of this directive is that humans are required or permitted to dominate nonhuman nature, that is, to use animals and plants for whatever purpose we wish, giving no independent weight at all to the interests of animals and plants. Another interpretation, however, understands dominion, not as domination, but as a caring stewardship toward nonhuman nature, which imposes limits on the ways that we can use animals and plants in pursuit of our own purposes, thereby making it possible for other living things to flourish.

Obviously, this second interpretation accords better with the perspective found in American Indian and other non-Western cultures. However, it is the first interpretation that is most widely accepted throughout Western culture. Given these conflicting interpretations of the Genesis story, it is clear that an appeal to the Bible is not going to be decisive in determining how anyone should treat nonhuman nature. Accordingly, we need to determine whether reason alone can provide any compelling grounds for thinking that we are superior to nonhuman nature in ways that would justify our domination of it. In Chapter 8, we took up this very question and argued on the basis of reason alone that there are no grounds for thinking that we are superior to nonhuman nature in ways that would justify our domination of it. If this argument is correct, then those of us within Western culture can learn an important lesson from American Indian culture. It is that the intrinsic value of nonhuman species places a significant constraint on how we pursue our own interests, a constraint that rules out our domination of nonhuman nature.

Using Confucius

A central problem in traditional ethics is how to get people to strongly identify themselves with particular groups, such as families, communities or nations, so that they will be more willing to act for the good of those groups while at the same time getting them to think critically about the groups to which they belong so as to avoid doing considerable harm to themselves and others when pursuing the interests of those groups. To accomplish this task, we do well to consult the work of the Chinese philosopher Confucius.

Kung Fu-Tzu or Confucius, his Latinized name, lived from 551 BC to 479 BC, about 150 years before Plato. He was not known to the Western world until the late sixteenth century when Jesuit missionaries, in an effort to convert Chinese rulers, steeped themselves in ancient Confucian literature and were overwhelmed by what they found.

Soon reports made their way back to Europe. Leibniz wrote that the Chinese surpassed Europeans in practical philosophy and recommended that Chinese missionaries be sent to Europe, and Voltaire declared that in morality Europeans "ought to become disciples" of the Chinese. Christian Wolff said of the Chinese that "in the Art of Governing, this Nation has ever surpassed all others without exception."[10] Confucius became known as the patron saint of the Enlightenment. The *Analects* is a collection of the sayings of Confucius, probably compiled by his students.

Confucius was remarkably successful as a teacher. Of the twenty-two students mentioned in the *Analects*, nine attained important government posts and a tenth turned one down. Moreover, his impact was far-reaching. For 2,500 years, he was "the Master" to all of China, and his influence continued even after the communist revolution, and is more in evidence today.

If we look to Confucius for help in understanding how we can get people to strongly identify themselves with particular groups and, at the same time, think critically about the groups to which they belong, we find two central concepts: *jen* and *li*.[11] *Jen* refers, most of the time, to the highest ethical ideal, including such qualities as concern for the well-being of others, filial piety, respect for elders, and the ability to endure adverse circumstances. *Li* originally referred to the rites of sacrifice to spirits and ancestors, but eventually it came to refer to all traditional and customary norms governing the relationship between people. In a number of places in the *Analects*, Confucius remarks on the intimate connection between *jen* and *li*. When asked about *jen* (in 12:1) Confucius says, "To return to the practice of *li* through the subduing of self constitutes *jen*." In 1:2, Confucius describes filial piety as the essential starting point for cultivating *jen*, and in another place filial piety is explained in terms of the observance of *li*.

These passages could lead us to interpret Confucius as an extreme traditionalist who advocated an uncritical acceptance of traditional and customary norms, but from what Confucius says elsewhere it is clear that he envisions *jen* as having a critical function with respect to *li*. For example, in 9:3, he says,

> A ceremonial cap of linen is what is prescribed by *li*. Today black silk is used instead. This is more frugal and I follow the majority. To prostrate oneself before ascending the steps (to enter the presence of the prince) is what is prescribed by *li*. Today one does so after having ascended them. This is casual and, though going against the majority, I follow the practice of doing so before ascending.
>
> The linen cap is that prescribed by the rules of ceremony, but now a silk one is worn. It is economical, and I follow the common practice. The rules of ceremony prescribe the bowing below the hall, but now the practice is to bow only after ascending it. That is arrogant. I continue to bow below the hall, [and thus] I oppose the common practice.

In this passage, Confucius is clearly evaluating two conflicts between current common practices and older rules, favoring the common practice in one case and an older rule in the other, in terms of their appropriateness for securing *jen*.

But how do we know when to abide by common or customary practices and when to depart from them? Sometimes this can be quite difficult to determine. In 13:18, the governor of She informs Confucius, "In our village there is one who may be styled upright in his conduct. When his father stole a sheep, he gave evidence against him." Confucius replies, "In our village, those who are upright are quite different. Fathers conceal the misconduct of their sons and sons conceal the misconduct of their fathers." But surely there are limits to the degree one should conceal the misconduct of one's relatives. It was surely appropriate for David Kaczynski to turn in his brother, the Unabomber, who over seventeen years had planted sixteen bombs at various locations in the United States, killing three and injuring twenty-nine people.[12]

Consider another case. In her book *Woman Warrior*, Maxine Hong Kingston retells a traditional Chinese ballad of a young woman who takes the place of her aged father when he is called into the army. Kingston juxtaposes the "perfect filiality" of the woman warrior with her own inability to win from her family or community any appreciation for her worldly achievements. She stresses how women's triumphs are often achieved in the face of familial or societal opposition. What these examples show is that it is not always easy to know when we should abide by the common or customary practices of our society and when we should depart from them. Clearly, much depends on what alternatives are actually available to us in the historical circumstances in which we find ourselves. After all, "ought" does imply "can," and so we cannot be morally required to do what it would be unreasonable to expect us to do. What this discussion of Confucian ethics shows, however, is that sometimes we need to rebel against common or customary practices and that sometimes we need to do so for the sake of traditional values themselves.

NEW OBLIGATIONS FOR TRADITIONAL ETHICS

In "Perversions of Justice: A Native-American Examination of the Doctrine of U.S. Rights to Occupancy in North America," American Indian activist Ward Churchill argues that the United States does not now possess, nor has it ever possessed, a legitimate right to occupancy in at least half the territory it claims as its own on this continent.[13] Certainly, this is not a widely held perspective in the United States. It certainly is not the perspective that is endorsed in the textbooks approved by the conservative state boards in Texas and California, which because of the size of their markets set the standard for textbook publishers across the United States. Nevertheless, if traditional ethics is to avoid bias against non-Western ideals, it must come to terms with Churchill's American Indian perspective, assessing what implications it has, if any, for our obligations to American Indians today. To do that, we need to take another look at the conquest of the American Indians by the Europeans who came to the New World.

Recent estimates put the Indian population of North and South America before the arrival of Columbus at around 100,000,000 with about 15,000,000 of these Indians living north of the Rio Grande. For comparison, the population of Europe at that time was about 70,000,000, the population of Russia about 18,000,000, and Africa about 72,000,000.

By the end of the sixteenth century, scholars estimate that about 200,000 Spaniards had moved to the Indies, to Mexico, and to Central and South America. Scholars also estimate that by that time between 60,000,000 and 80,000,000 natives from those lands had died primarily due to disease but also due to the harsh treatment they received at the hands of the Spaniards.

While fewer Indians lived north of the Rio Grande, the prevailing British, and later American, attitude to these Indians was, if anything, harsher than that of the Spaniards. What the British, and later the Americans, wanted was land—the very same land that the Indians occupied. As Edward Waterhouse, a Jamestown settler, put it,

> We shall enjoy their cultivated places ... [and] their cleared grounds in all their villages (which are situated in the fruitfullest places of the land) shall be inhabited by us.[14]

Specifically, the goal was to either push the Indians westward or exterminate them.

This goal was clearly endorsed at the highest levels of society. In 1779, George Washington ordered Major General John Sullivan to attack the Iroquois and "lay waste all the settlements around ... that the country may not be merely overrun but destroyed," urging the general not to "listen to any overture of peace before the total ruin of their settlements is effected."[15] Surviving Indians referred to Washington by the nickname "Town Destroyer" because under his direct orders twenty-eight out of thirty Seneca towns from Lake Erie to the Mohawk River and *all* the towns and villages of the Mohawk, the Onondaga, and the Cayuga were totally obliterated. As one surviving Iroquois told Washington to his face in 1792,

> To this day, when that name is heard, our women look behind them and turn pale, and our children cling close to the necks of their mother.[16]

This goal of removal or extermination was also shared by Adams, Monroe, and Jefferson. For example, Jefferson instructed his secretary of state in 1807 that any Indians who resisted American expansion must be met with "the hatchet." "And ... if ever we are constrained to lift the hatchet against any tribe," he wrote, "we will never lay it down till that tribe is exterminated, or driven beyond the Mississippi," adding that "in war, they will kill some of us, [but] we shall destroy all of them."[17]

In 1828, Andrew Jackson, who had once written that "the whole Cherokee nation ought to be scourged," was elected president of the United States.[18] Jackson supported the state of Georgia's attempt to appropriate a large portion of Cherokee land. When the U.S. Supreme Court ruled against Jackson and the state of Georgia, Jackson had a treaty drawn up ceding the Cherokee lands to the American government in exchange for money and some land in the Indian Territory of Oklahoma. With the most influential leader of the Cherokees imprisoned and their tribal printing press shut down by the government, a treaty was negotiated with certain "cooperative" Cherokees. Yet even the American military officer who was to register the tribe's members for removal protested that this treaty was,

> ... no treaty at all, because [it was] not sanctioned by the great body of the Cherokee and [it was] made without their participation or assent. I solemnly declare to you that upon its reference to the Cherokee people it would be instantly rejected by nine-tenths of them, and I believe by nineteen-twentieths of them.[19]

With this treaty signed, the members of the Cherokee nation were force-marched overland to the Indian Territory, intentionally passing through areas where it was known that cholera and other epidemic diseases were raging. Thus, of the 17,000 who began the march, called by the Indians the Trail of Tears, only 9,000 arrived in Oklahoma.

Actually, in the West itself, extermination of the Indians, rather than relocation, seemed to be the preferred policy. For example, Colonel John Chivington, who led 700 armed soldiers in a massacre of mostly women and children at Sand Creek in Colorado in 1864, announced earlier that he wanted his troops to "kill and scalp all, little and big," noting that "nits make lice."[20] And in 1867, when Tosawi, a Chief of the Comanches, introduced himself to General Philip Sheridan with "Tosawi, good Indian," Sheridan responded with his often-quoted remark, "The only good Indians I ever saw were dead."[21]

There is little doubt that Chivington's and Sheridan's views were widely shared. For example, Oliver Wendel Holmes claimed that Indians were nothing more than a "half-filled outline of humanity" whose "extermination" was the necessary "solution to the problem of [their] relation to the white race."[22] Similarly, William Dean Howells took "patriotic pride" in advocating "the extermination of the red savages of the plains."[23] And Theodore Roosevelt maintained that the extermination of the American Indians and the expropriation of their lands "was as ultimately beneficial as it was inevitable."[24] In Texas, an official bounty on native scalps—*any* native scalp—was maintained well into the 1870s.

In 1890, the U.S. government declared the period of conquest called "Indian Wars" to be officially over. At that time, it also determined that only 248,253 Indians remained alive within its borders, with another 122,585 residing in Canada. This represented a 98 percent decline from pre-Columbian times.

In the final stages of the European conquest, American Indian children were taken from their parents at early ages, sent to boarding schools, and educated in "white" ways. As the director of one of these schools put it, the goal was to "kill the Indian ... and save the man."[25] In 1887, more than fourteen thousand Indian children were enrolled in such boarding schools. When the students eventually returned to their reservations, they were virtual strangers, unable to speak their own language or understand the ways of their people.

Nor were these atrocities in any way compensated for by way of providing American Indians with good opportunities to develop themselves and become respectable members of society. Currently, the poverty rate on American Indian reservations in the United States is almost four times the national average, and on some reservations, such as Pine Ridge in South Dakota and Tohomo O'Odham in Arizona (where more than 60 percent of homes are without adequate plumbing, compared with 2 percent for the nation at large), the poverty rate is nearly five times the national average. While a number of Indian groups whose reservations are located near population centers have been able to better themselves by operating casinos, on the Pine Ridge Reservation, the average life expectancy is 50 years, compared to the average life expectancy of 77.5 years in the United States as a whole. On Pine Ridge Reservation, the teenage suicide rate is also 400 percent higher than the national average for the same age group and the infant mortality rate is 500 percent higher than the national average. The destitution and ill health that prevails on many reservations today is similar to conditions in the Third World.[26] American Indians today suffer not only from alienation but from extreme social and economic injustice as well.

If we compare the conquest of the American Indians with the Holocaust in Europe, two aspects stand out. First, a greater number of American Indians lost their lives during the European conquest of North and South America than did Jews during the Holocaust 74,000,000–94,000,000 American Indians compared to 6,000,000 Jews. Second, not only were many Indian tribes, like the Jews, threatened with extinction, but many Indian tribes were actually driven into extinction; for example, in the state of Texas alone, the once populous Karankawa, Akokisa, Bidui, Tejas, and Coahuiltans are now all extinct.

There is also an interesting historical connection between the two evils. The conquest of the American Indians began first, but it, in turn was affected by events in Spain. In 1492, as Columbus set sail for the New World, Jews, ultimately 120,000 to 150,000, were being deported from Spain, and, on subsequent trips, Columbus brought with him heavily armed and armored infantry and cavalry fresh from their victory over the Moors in Granada. The Spaniards were ready to conquer the New World, and conquer it they did by massacring, enslaving, and decimating all the groups of Indians with whom they came in contact.

Subsequently, however, in the twentieth century, the treatment of the American Indians was used by Nazi leaders to justify inflicting the Holocaust on the Jews. According to Hitler,

> Neither Spain nor Britain should be models of German expansion, but the Nordics of North America, who had ruthlessly pushed aside an inferior race to win for themselves soil and territory for the future.[27]

Similarly, Heinrich Himmler explained to a confidant that he knew that the Final Solution would mean much suffering for the Jews. But he pointed to what the Americans had done earlier, which was to exterminate the Indians—who wanted only to go on living on their native land—in the most abominable way.[28]

So what should be the response of traditional ethics to the conquest of the American Indians—what has been called the American Holocaust? What implications do these past events have for our obligations to American Indians today? Should the United States give a sizable chunk of its land back to the American Indians in view of its history of past injustices?

That is exactly what Ward Churchill argues should be done.[29] He notes that the United States entered into and ratified over 370 separate treaties with various tribes of American Indians over the first ninety years of its existence. Of course, a number of these ratified treaties were fraudulent or coerced. Sometimes, the United States appointed its own preferred Indian "leaders" to represent their tribes in negotiating the treaties. In at least one case—the Treaty of Fort Wise—the U.S. negotiators appear to have forged the signatures of various Cheyenne and Arapaho leaders. There are also about 400 other treaties that were never ratified by the U.S. Senate and so were never legally binding, but upon which the United States now claims legal title to appreciable portions of North America. Yet even if we assume, just for the sake of argument, that all these treaties are legally and morally binding—something we know is not the case—it still turns out, according to the federal government's own study, that the United States has no legal basis whatsoever—no treaty, no agreement, not even an arbitrary act of Congress—to fully one-third of the area within the lower forty-eight states (the legal claims to Alaska and Hawaii are even more tenuous).

Churchill points out that because the federal and state governments together still own between 45 and 47 percent of the continental United States, it is possible to restore to American Indian tribes 30 percent of the continental landmass, thus restoring to them roughly the percentage of land to which the United States itself admits it has no clear legal title, without evicting any non-Indian homeowners from their land.

Churchill goes on to propose a more specific plan for how this is to be done.[30] Drawing on the work of Frank and Deborah Popper at Rutgers University, he notes that there are 110 counties within the Great Plains region that have been fiscally insolvent since the time they were taken away from Indian tribes more than a century ago. This is an area of about 140,000 square miles inhabited by a widely dispersed non-Indian population of around 400,000. Without continual federal subsidies, none of these counties would be viable.

What the Poppers proposed is that the government cut its perpetual losses and buy back the individual holdings within these counties, giving the land back to American Indian tribes as a Buffalo Commons. Churchill goes further.[31] He notes that there are another hundred or so counties adjoining the "perpetual red ink" counties that are economically marginal, and suggests that these counties, along with national grasslands in Wyoming and national forests and parklands in the Black Hills, could be added to the Buffalo Commons. He also suggests that this Commons could be extended westward to include Indian reservations and other sparsely populated and economically insolvent regions until it constitutes roughly one-third of the continental United States. It could then be recognized as a sort of North American Union of Indigenous Nations.

So what are we to think of Churchill's plan for restoring Indian lands? If traditional ethics is to adequately take into account the conquest of the American Indians, would it not have to recognize an obligation to restore Indian lands, and would that not lead to endorsing either a proposal for a Buffalo Commons or a North American Union of Indigenous Nations? If this would not be required, what would be required? A substantial outlay of economic resources to lift every American Indian out of poverty? Greater authority to open casinos and other tax-free businesses? Whatever is specifically required in order for traditional ethics to adequately take into account an American Indian perspective, it will surely involve recognizing obligations to American Indians that we have not recognized or fully recognized before.

APPLYING TRADITIONAL ETHICS CROSS-CULTURALLY

Yet even when traditional ethics does not need to be corrected or reinterpreted in light of non-Western ideals, or when knowledge of non-Western cultures is not needed to recognize obligations that we either did not recognize or fully recognize before, it still is the case that knowledge of non-Western cultures is required to properly apply traditional ethics. Failing to consider the relevant local culture or cultures when applying traditional ethics can lead to disastrous results. A well-known example of this sort of failure is the U.S. involvement in Vietnam.

The U.S. involvement in Vietnam began as support for France's efforts to retake its former colony at the end of World War II. Unfortunately, the decision to help France retake Vietnam was made with little knowledge of Vietnamese history and culture or the background and character of Ho Chi Minh and the Viet Minh. For example, Franklin Delano Roosevelt once commented that the Vietnamese were a people of "small stature and not warlike."[32] He and other American leaders were unaware of Vietnam's thousand-year struggle against the Chinese and Mongols and its defeat of the fearsome Genghis Khan, nor did they know about the Vietnamese generals who, centuries before Mao Tse-tung, pioneered the art of guerrilla warfare.

Vietnamese recorded history began in 207 BC[33] On that date, Trieu Da, a Chinese war lord, declared himself ruler of a large area encompassing southern China and Vietnam, as far south as present-day Danang. The informal name of this region was "Nam Viet" meaning "land of the southern Viets." Trieu Da ruled his Vietnamese domains indirectly, leaving Viet feudal lords in charge of local affairs. In 111 BC, Wu-ti, the great Han Emperor, conquered Nam Viet. It became a province within the Chinese empire, and for the next thousand years, the northern half of present-day Vietnam was controlled by the Chinese. During this long period of colonial rule, while the Vietnamese adopted many features of Chinese culture, they continued to resist Chinese political domination and economic exploitation.

It took the Vietnamese a millennium to finally win their independence from China in 938. During the next near millennium, until the arrival of the French in the 1850s, every new dynasty that came to power in China invaded Vietnam. These wars with China helped to make central to Vietnamese military thought the idea that an ostensibly weaker force, properly handled, can defeat a stronger one. This idea is hardly new, but the Vietnamese did much to refine it. Vietnamese military teaching emphasized that a more powerful enemy had to be worn down by protracted warfare. Hit-and-run tactics, delaying actions, ambush, and harassment by guerrilla bands were to be employed. Finally, when the enemy was sufficiently drained and demoralized, he was to be finished off by a sudden offensive delivered with maximum surprise and deception.

On August 15, 1945, the same day that Emperor Hirohito announced the surrender of his country over Radio Tokyo, Ho Chi Minh, the leader of the Viet

Minh (the Vietnamese Independence Brotherhood League), had his representative in Kunming, China, send President Truman a message through the American Office of Strategic Services (OSS) station there asking "the United States, as a champion of democracy" to make Vietnam an American protectorate "on the same status as the Philippines for an undetermined period" before full independence. He received no reply. Two weeks later, in Hanoi, with American OSS officers in attendance and a Vietnamese band playing "The Star-Spangled Banner," Ho proclaimed the Republic of Vietnam independent before a crowd of 500,000 assembled in Ba Dinh Square. Ho's declaration, echoing the famous phrases and the political ideals of the American Declaration of Independence, read as follows:

> All men are created equal. They are endowed by their Creator with certain unalienable rights, among these are Life, Liberty and the Pursuit of Happiness.... These are undeniable Truths.
>
> Nevertheless, for more than eighty years, the French imperialists, abusing the standard of Liberty, Equality and Fraternity, have violated our Fatherland and oppressed our fellow citizens. Their acts are the opposite of the ideals of humanity and justice.
>
> In the field of politics, they deprived us of all liberties. They have enforced inhuman laws ... they have built more prisons than schools. They have mercilessly slain our patriots; they have drowned our uprisings in rivers of blood.
>
> We are convinced that the Allies who recognized the principle of equality of all the peoples at the Conferences of Teheran and San Francisco cannot but recognize the independence of Vietnam.
>
> Vietnam has the right to be [a] free and independent country; and in fact is so already.[34]

Altogether Ho sent Truman and Truman's first secretary of state James Byrnes, eleven telegrams and letters of appeal over the eighteen-month period after his establishment of a Vietnamese government in Hanoi. None of these communications were acknowledged. Ho made similar pleas for rescue to Clement Attlee, the prime minister of Britain, to Generalissimo Chiang Kai-shek of Nationalist China, and to Joseph Stalin of the Soviet Union. They too did not answer. Thus, Ho and the Viet Minh began their fight against the French in 1945 without any outside help whatsoever. Aid from China came only at the end of 1949 following the victory of Mao Tse-tung over Chiang Kai-shek. Soviet aid to the Viet Minh did not begin until the 1950s. This determination of Ho Chi Minh and the Viet Minh to fight the French on their own should have convinced American decision makers that they were no pawns of the Chinese and the Soviets. They should have recognized Ho Chi Minh and General Giap as belonging to a long history of Vietnamese nationalists who believed that they could defeat more powerful invaders of their land because their ancestors had done so many times before. Unfortunately, ignorance of Vietnamese history and culture and the background and character of Ho Chi Minh and the Viet Minh led American decision makers to support the wrong public policy with disastrous results. The mistake was a fundamental one. To arrive at the right public policies, traditional ethics must take into account the relevant local culture or cultures. The failure of U.S. involvement in Vietnam should have burned this lesson deeply in the minds of future U.S leaders.

Sadly, this did not happen, at least with regard to the U.S. invasion of Iraq in 2003.[35] Before ordering the invasion, George W. Bush and the members of his administration clearly failed to adequately inform themselves about the history and local cultures of Iraq. They thought that they could quickly overthrow Saddam Hussein, disband the Iraqi army, dissolve the Ba'ath party which ran the state, bring to power a secular Iraqi exile like Ahmed Chalabi, and then start to remove their forces from Iraq just three months after the collapse of Saddam's regime.[36] Bush and the members never expected the ethnic and religious violence that erupted between Sunni and Shiite groups nor the influx into the country of Islamic extremists following the overthrow of Saddam Hussein. Of course, a correct application of moral principles would never have justified the U.S.-led invasion of Iraq in the first place. Nevertheless, that serious mistake was only further compounded by the Bush administration's woeful ignorance of the history and cultures of the people of Iraq on whom it sought to impose its will.

Conclusion

In this chapter, it has been argued that to meet the challenge of multiculturalism, we must defend an ethics that is secular in character and one that can survive a wide-ranging comparative evaluation of both Western and non-Western moral ideals. It has been further argued that there are at least three ways that non-Western cultures can contribute to fashioning an ethics of this sort. First, non-Western moral ideals can help to significantly correct or interpret our Western moral ideals themselves. Second, non-Western cultures can help us recognize important obligations that flow from our moral ideals that we either did not recognize or fully recognize before. Third, non-Western cultures can help us know how best to apply our own moral ideals, especially cross-culturally. With respect to each of these claims, the argument in this chapter has been, of necessity, by way of example, drawing on Confucian ethics, American Indian culture and perspectives, Vietnamese history and culture, and Iraqi history and culture to indicate, in specific ways, how traditional ethics can meet the challenge of multiculturalism. Obviously, more work of this sort needs to be done. It is the only way we can have a defensible ethics.

MySearchLab Connections

Watch. Listen. Explore. Read. MySearchLab is designed just for you. Each chapter features a customized study plan to help you learn key concepts and terms. Dynamic visual activities, videos, and readings found in the multimedia library will enhance your learning experience.

Here are a few questions and activities to help you understand this chapter:

1. How is the multicultural challenge to traditional Western ethics rooted in the history of colonialism (p. 122)?

   Read "Colonialism," Multimedia Library, Web Resources, Stanford Encyclopedia of Philosophy.

2. What else can traditional Western ethics learn from Confucius (p. 126)?

   Read "Confucius," Multimedia Library, Web Resources, Internet Encyclopedia of Philosophy.

Each chapter features a customized study plan to help you learn and review key concepts and terms.

Notes

1. Quoted in Mary Louise Pratt, "Humanities for the Future: Reflections on the Western Culture Debate at Stanford," in the *Politics of Liberal Education*, ed. Daryl Gless and Barbara Hernstein Smith (Durham: Duke University Press, 1992), 25.

2. Ibid.

3. Ibid., 15.

4. Now there are other ways to interpret the challenge of multiculturalism to traditional ethics. In this chapter, we will interpret it as a challenge that comes from non-Western cultures. One might also interpret it as a challenge that also comes from, for example, feminist culture, gay and lesbian culture, or class culture. Here we will set aside these other challenges since they are often considered in order to give the challenge to traditional ethics that comes from non-Western cultures the attention it deserves.

5. Quoted in Karen Warren, "The Power and Promise of Ecological Feminism," in *Earth Ethics,* 2nd ed., ed. James P. Sterba (Upper Saddle River, NJ: Prentice Hall, 2000).

6. Edward Curtis, *Native American Wisdom* (Philadelphia: Temple University Press, 1993), 87.

7. Luther Standing Bear, *Land of the Spotted Eagle* (Boston: Houghton Mifflin, 1933), 45.

8. Jorge Valadez, "Pre-Columbian Philosophical Perspectives," in *Ethics: Classical Western Texts in Feminist and Multicultural Perspectives*, ed. James P. Sterba (New York: Oxford University Press, 2000), 106–8.

9. Gen. 1:28.

10. Quoted in H. G. Creel, *Confucius: The Man and the Myth* (Westport, CT: Greenwood Press, 1972).

11. See David Wong, "Community, Diversity, and Confucianism," in *In The Company of Others*, ed. Nancy Snow (Lanham, MD: Rowman and Littlefield, 1996), 17–37; Russell Fox, "Confucian and Communitarian Responses," *The Review of Politics* (1997): 561–92.
12. Maria Eftimiades, "Blood Bond," *People,* August 10, 1998, 4, 77.
13. Ward Churchill, "Perversions of Justice: A Native-American Examination of the Doctrine of U.S. Rights to Occupancy in North America," in *Ethics: Classical Western Texts in Feminist and Multicultural Perspectives*, ed. James P. Sterba (New York: Oxford University Press, 2000), 401–18.
14. David Stannard, *American Holocaust* (New York: Oxford University Press, 1992), 106.
15. Ibid., 119.
16. Ibid., 120.
17. Ibid., 332.
18. Ibid., 121ff.
19. Ibid., 122; Michael Paul Rogin, *Fathers and Children: Andrew Jackson and the Subjugation of the American Indians* (New York: Alfred A. Knopf 1975), 227.
20. Stannard, *American Holocaust*, 131.
21. Dee Brown, *Bury My Heart at Wounded Knee* (New York: Henry Holt and Co., 1970), 170.
22. Stannard, *American Holocaust*, 245.
23. Ibid.; William Dean Howells, "A Sennight of the Contennial," *Atlantic Monthly* 38 (July 1876): 103.
24. Quoted in Thomas G. Dyer, *Theodore Roosevelt and the Idea of Race* (Baton Rouge: Louisiana State University Press, 1980), 78.
25. Sharon O'Brien, *American Tribal Governments* (Norman: University of Oklahoma Press, 1989), 76.
26. Stannard, *American Holocaust*, 256–57; Stephanie M. Schwartz, "The Arrogance of Ignorance: Hidden Away, Out of Sight and Out of Mind," *Link Center Foundation* (2006), http://www.linkcenterfoundation.org/id24.html.
27. See Adolf Hitler, *Hitler's Secret Book*, trans. Salvator Attanasio (New York: Grove Press, 1961), 44–48.
28. Roger Manvell and Heinrich Fraenkel, *The Comparable Crime* (New York: G. P. Putnam's Sons, 1967), 45.
29. Ward Churchill, *The Struggle for the Land* (Monroe, ME: Common Courage Press, 1993), Part IV.
30. Ibid.
31. Ibid.
32. See Sandra Taylor, "Vietnam in the Beginning," *Reviews in American History* (1989): 308.
33. George Moss, *Vietnam: An American Ordeal*, 3rd ed. (Upper Saddle River, NJ: Prentice Hall, 1990), Chapter 1; Niel Sheehan, *A Bright Shining Lie* (New York: Random House, 1988), Book II.
34. George Moss, *A Vietnam Reader* (Upper Saddle River, NJ: Prentice Hall, 1991), 32–34.
35. Anthony H. Cordesman, "American Strategic and Tactical Failure in Iraq: An Update," *Center of Strategic and International Studies* (Washington, DC: CSIS, 2006), 1–14.
36. Except, of course, for a few well-placed military bases. See Ibid.

CONCLUSION

The promise of this book was that it would help you make the ethical choices that you confront in your lives. Now it is time for you to determine how successful this book has been in that endeavor. Consider what this book has done for you.

THREE CHALLENGES

This book began by addressing three important challenges to the very possibility of ethics, providing an independent source of the knowledge needed for making ethical choices. The views of the divine command theorist (morality is determined simply by the commands of God) and the ethical relativist (morality is determined simply by the demands of culture) were given their day in court and found wanting. In both cases, the normative requirements of human nature and the circumstances of our lives were seen to provide an independent source of morality; God and culture can go beyond the normative requirements of human nature and the circumstances of our lives, but they can't go against them. Torturing innocent people simply for the fun of it, for example, was seen as not something that either God or culture can make morally right to do.

Egoism too provided a significant challenge to ethics. Not content with simply denying the independent status of morality, egoism challenged the very existence of moral requirements. It claimed that either all that we can do (Psychological Egoism) or all that we should do (Ethical Egoism) is just serve our own self-interest. Yet it too, given its day in court, was found wanting. Morality was shown to be possible (thus defeating Psychological Egoism) as well as rationally preferable to Ethical Egoism.

THREE CONCEPTIONS OF ETHICS

That still left the problem of how best to interpret ethics. Traditionally, ethics has been given utilitarian, Kantian, and Aristotelian interpretations. We then evaluated each of these interpretations.

Utilitarian ethics requires us to always choose whatever action or social policy would have the best consequences for everyone concerned. We tested this view out to see whether it would recommend the torture favored by former vice president Cheney or the terrorism favored by Osama bin Laden. We discovered that rarely, if ever, would such actions be justified, given that there would almost always be other ways to achieve the desired results without using such objectionable means, or because these means themselves would fail to satisfy an expanded "Ought" implies "Can" principle that internally constrains what utilitarian ethics can require.

Kantian ethics requires us to test our behavior by asking, in effect, what if everyone did that, and then rejecting those actions that cannot be so universalized. We experimented with this Kantian test by applying it to different possible rules for keeping promises and saw the need to build into the test morally appropriate exceptions to otherwise approved rules. As in the case of utilitarian ethics, it also made sense to regard Kantian ethics as internally constrained by an expanded "Ought" implies "Can" principle.

Aristotelian ethics specifies moral requirements in terms of the virtuous life, which is further determined by what a person at a particular stage of development should do next in order to become more virtuous. We considered Ayn Rand's interpretation of Aristotelian ethics that requires us to make a virtue of selfishness. We found that the Rand's thesis that the people's rational interests don't conflict, which is needed to support her self-centered ethics, is contradicted by the lives of main characters from her own novels, especially by the arch-villain, Ellsworth Toohey. Moreover, once that no-conflict thesis is abandoned, it became evident that, just as in utilitarian ethics and Kantian ethics, conflict of interest in Aristotelian ethics need to be resolved in accord with an expanded "Ought" implies "Can" principle.

As we noted in the Taking-Stock Interlude, given the ways that utilitarian ethics, Kantian ethics, and Aristotelian ethics have been specified to make them morally defensible, including being constrained by an expanded "Ought" implies "Can" principle, there is little reason to think that they would not all favor the very same practical requirements.

THREE MORE CHALLENGES

Still, there is a problem. Traditional ethics, as we saw, whether utilitarian, Kantian or Aristotelian, has itself been challenged as morally defective. These challenges come from environmentalism, feminism, and multiculturalism, and they must be met if traditional ethics is to be useful in helping us make ethically defensible choices.

The environmental challenge that traditional ethics is biased against nonhuman living beings took several forms—a utilitarian challenge developed by Peter Singer; a Kantian challenge developed by Tom Regan; and a more general, and arguably more morally adequate biocentric challenge pioneered by Paul Taylor, which requires that traditional ethics take into account the interests of all nonhuman living beings. It was argued that in order to best meet this challenge, by taking into account the interests of all nonhuman living beings, traditional ethics needs to subscribe to a set of conflict resolution principles that appropriately weigh the conflicting interests of humans and nonhuman living beings so as to best resolve those conflicts.

The feminist challenge that there is a male bias in traditional ethics was exemplified by the failure of John Rawls's theory of justice to adequately take the interests of women into account, and by the general failure of Kantian, utilitarian, and Aristotelian ethical theories to adequately take the interests of women in account when specifying their ideals of a morally good person. Yet such failures are correctable. Traditional ethics can use their theories of justice and their ideals of a morally good person to determine just family structures and to defend an ideal of androgyny which makes all truly desirable traits that can be distributed in society equally open to both women and men.

The multicultural challenge maintained that there is a Western bias in traditional ethics. Its central claim is that if Western moral ideals are to be defensible, they must be able to survive a comparative evaluation with other moral ideals, including non-Western ones. Yet, unfortunately, traditional ethics has simply ignored the need for a comparative evaluation of this sort, resting content on an evaluation that is limited to Western moral ideals, usually the utilitarian, Kantian, and Aristotelian perspectives discussed in previous chapters. We were then able to show how by using examples drawn from American Indian culture, Confucian ethics, the history of what has been called "the American Holocaust," Ho Chi Minh and the Vietnam War, and the U.S. invasion of Iraq and the overthrow of Saddam Hussein, non-Western cultures can contribute the fashioning of a defensible ethics for our times.

In this way, traditional ethics, whether utilitarian, Kantian or Aristotelian, when suitably modified, is shown to be able to meet the challenges of feminism, environmentalism, and multiculturalism, and thus maintain its usefulness for helping us make the ethical choices we face in our lives.

PRACTICING ETHICS

But how does it do this? Consider a range of moral issues concerning which you will most surely be required to take a stand.

1. The distribution of income and wealth
2. Torture and terrorism
3. Abortion and euthanasia
4. Genetic engineering
5. Gay and lesbian concerns
6. Work and family responsibilities
7. Women's and men's roles
8. Affirmative action
9. Pornography
10. Sexual harassment
11. Punishment
12. War and humanitarian intervention

Now with respect to each of these issues, let us see how the resources of this book can help you in resolving them.

ISSUE I

The issue of distribution of income and wealth was first raised in the Introduction when we considered that the poverty rate on American Indian reservations is almost four times the national average, and how on Pine Ridge Reservation in

South Dakota, conditions are even worse. We also noted in the Interlude, that when Aristotelian ethics, Kantian ethics, and utilitarian ethics are all given their most morally defensible interpretations, and thus constrained by an expanded "Ought" implies "Can" principle, there is no reason to think that they would not favor the same resolution of this moral issue as they would of any other. Accordingly, to resolve this particular issue, we would need to especially take into account the conflicting perspectives of the rich and the poor in our society, and we would need more data about the rich and the poor and the availability of economic resources in our society before we can come up with a morally defensible resolution of this issue. Still, using the information and the common moral framework already at our disposal, we are not far from a morally defensible resolution of this issue.

We may even not be too far from a resolution when the issue is expanded to include the worldwide distribution of income and wealth as well. This is because at the heart of the matter there remains the conflict between the poor and the rich, now just seen in a broader setting. Without a doubt, more information about the availability of economic resources worldwide would surely be needed to reach an appropriate resolution of the issue. But even with the partial information we now have, we are probably not without our hunches about what a morally defensible resolution would turn out to be like.

ISSUE 2

With regard to the moral issues of torture and terrorism, the discussion in Chapter 4 is probably the most relevant. Again, more information and argument would be required to properly resolve these issues. Nevertheless, it seems fairly clear that rarely, if ever, would acts of torture or terror be morally justified given that there would almost always be other ways to achieve the desired results without using such objectionable means. In addition, such means would surely tend to fail to satisfy an expanded "Ought" implies "Can" principle that internally constrains, not just utilitarian ethics, but Kantian ethics and Aristotelian ethics as well. Nevertheless, there may be exceptions, and that is why a careful examination of this issue, particularly in international contexts—one that takes into account both Western and non-Western perspectives—is required.

ISSUES 3, 4, AND 5

Obviously, the issues of abortion, euthanasia, genetic engineering, and gay and lesbian concerns, each require its own particular discussion where the issue is clarified, relevant information is provided, and practical alternatives are discussed for resolving the issue. There is, however, one very important contribution that this book does make to such discussions. It is that the resolution of each of these particular issues, involving enforcement as it does, must be justified with sufficient reasons that are accessible to all those to whom it applies. This is because, as was argued in Chapter 1, people cannot be justifiably forced to abide by ethical requirements if they cannot come to know, and so come to justifiably believe, that they should abide by those requirements. For an ethics to justifiably enforce its requirements, there must be sufficient reasons accessible to all those to whom it applies to abide by those requirements. What this means is that the ethics must be secular rather than religious in character because only secular reasons are accessible to everyone; religious reasons are primarily accessible only to the members of the particular religious groups who hold them, and as such they cannot provide the justification that is needed to support the enforcement of the basic requirements of morality with regard to abortion, euthanasia, genetic engineering, and gay and lesbian concerns, or with regard to any other issue involving enforcement.

ISSUES 6 AND 7

The issues of work and family responsibilities and women's and men's roles and traits were discussed in some detail in Chapter 8 in connection with the feminist challenge to traditional ethics. More information and argument is surely required to fully resolve these issues, but we have also noted that this is a neglected area of discussion in traditional ethics, and so this neglect must be remedied if the feminist challenge is to be met. Nevertheless, we are aware of the general direction a proper resolution of these issues would take. Thus, to deal with the first issue, an account of what would be just family structures seems to be required, and to deal with the second, we seem to need to move toward a deeper ideal of equal opportunity that makes all truly desirable traits that can be distributed in society equally open to both women and men.

ISSUES 8, 9, AND 10

In addressing the issues of affirmative action, pornography, and sexual harassment, it is helpful that this book provides alternative moral approaches that lead to the same practical requirements, but that still leaves a lot to be done if we are to figure out what are appropriate moral resolutions of each of these issues.

For example, there are different kinds of affirmative action—outreach, remedial, and diversity—with different justifications, and even the harshest critics of affirmative action, like Carl Cohen, don't reject all of them. So we have to learn more about the different forms of affirmative action and their proposed justifications before we can properly resolve this issue.

Similarly, there are different types of pornography. The distinction between hard-core and soft-core is widely recognized, but feminist critics of pornography also attempt to distinguish pornography from what they call "erotica," defined as "sexually explicit materials premised on equality" of which they approve![1] So here again, these complexities will have to be taken into account, along with the resources of this book, before we can reach a morally defensible resolution of the issue.

There is also considerable disagreement concerning what constitutes sexual harassment. Consider the following. A woman complained about her workplace where pictures of nude and scantily clad women abounded (including one, which hung on a wall for eight years, of a woman with a golf ball on her breasts and a man with his golf club standing over her and yelling "Fore!") and where a coworker, never disciplined despite repeated complaints, routinely referred to women as "whores," "cunts," "pussies," and "tits."[2] Was this sexual harassment? Most people, I believe, think that it was, but the court ruling in this case found it not a sufficiently hostile environment to constitute sexual harassment! So we would definitely need to consider a variety of relevant cases in order to determine what should be considered to be sexual harassment and how we should best prevent it.

Thus, with respect to the issues of affirmative action, pornography, and sexual harassment, this book does provides a useful moral framework for taking up the issues, but additional resources are clearly needed in order to determine what ought to be done with respect to each issue.

ISSUE 11

At first, addressing the issue of punishment in a society looks quite straightforward. All we seemingly need to do is determine who is responsible for what crimes and then determine what their punishment should be. Of course, we would need to gather data on the crimes that are committed in a society and the punishments that are usually imposed. But having that, we could seemingly determine the appropriateness of the punishment to the crime.

Unfortunately, there is a serious problem with doing this. It arises because many of the crimes that are committed in a society are property crimes where someone, say Anna, takes something to which someone else, say Pedro, has a legal property right to what Anna takes. But what if the distribution of property, which, of course, is virtually equivalent to the distribution of income and wealth, is unjust? Suppose then that what Anna takes from Pedro is something to which she would be legally entitled to in a just society, but something to which she is not legally entitled in the unjust society in which both she and Pedro live.

How then could Anna be legitimately punished for doing what she would be morally entitled to do in a just society? It would seem that she could not. In this way, we can see that at least for property crimes, the moral justification for punishment in a society depends on whether there is a moral justification for the distribution of property (or the distribution of income and wealth) in that society. The moral justification of the criminal justice system, at least with respect to property, depends on the moral justification of the distributive justice system that determines who has legal entitlement to property. If the distributive justice system lacks moral justification, then so does the criminal justice system. Clearly, this is a useful and challenging way to approach the issue of punishment, relating it to the proper distribution of income and wealth, an issue with which this book does bring you quite close to a resolution.

ISSUE 12

The multicultural challenge to traditional ethics developed in Chapter 9 is probably the most relevant for addressing the moral issues of war and humanitarian intervention. In that chapter, examples were cited in which the United States, at different times, fueled by Western cultural biases, went to war against American Indians, North Vietnamese under Ho Chi Minh, and the Iraqis under Saddam Hussein. In each case, cultural biases led to serious moral failings. Hence, the main recommendation of this book with regard to the issue of war and humanitarian intervention is that Western powers, in particular, need to be far more careful than they have been in the past so that their cultural biases do not lead them into future military actions that are morally indefensible.

SUMMING-UP

As this survey of the twelve moral issues shows, this book does provide you with some very helpful suggestions for resolving these and other moral issues for yourself. That was its goal.

Yet perhaps you want more help. Well, it can be found by using *Introducing Ethics*, in conjunction with a moral issues reader that will provide you with additional data and arguments useful for resolving each of these and other practical issues. If you found *Introducing Ethics* helpful, a moral issues reader will help you build on what you have learned by providing additional resources. Used together, these two books should greatly increase your ability to resolve the moral issues you face in our times.

Notes

1. Catharine MacKinnon, "Pornography, Civil Rights, and Speech," *Harvard Civil Liberties Law Review* (1985).
2. *Christoforou v. Ryder Truck Rental*, 668 F. Supp. 294 (S.D.N.Y. 1987).

GLOSSARY

Androgyny: An ideal requiring that all human traits that are truly desirable and distributable in society be equally open to both women and men or, in the case of virtues, equally expected of both women and men, other things being equal.

Animal liberation: The goal of freeing animals from human exploitation.

Basic and luxury needs: Basic needs, if not satisfied, lead to significant lacks or deficiencies with respect to a standard of mental and physical well-being. Thus, a person's needs for food, shelter, medical care, protection, companionship, and self-development are, at least in part, needs of this sort. Luxury needs are those needs that are not basic needs.

Biocentrism: The view that all living beings have moral status which requires that we treat them in ways that are morally defensible. See: **Moral status**.

Categorical Imperative: The Categorical Imperative requires that we act only on maxims that we can at the same time will to be universal laws of nature (Kant). See: **Universalizability**.

Confucianism: An ethical doctrine developed by Confucius (551–479 BC) that emphasized proper, hierarchical relations between ruler and ruled, father and son, husband and wife, and the old and the young.

Divine command theory: The view that morality is fundamentally dependent on religion, or put in terms of the Euthyphro Question, that actions are right because God commanded them.

Euthyphro Question: This question asks whether actions are right because God commanded them or whether God commanded them to be done because they are right.

Gender roles and traits: Social roles and traits that are generally expected of a person on the basis of his or her sex.

General revelation: The knowledge of God's commands that is made possible through observation of the natural world and through reflections on human experiences that are universal and commonly accessible.

Geneva Conventions: A series of agreements first formulated at an international convention held in Geneva, Switzerland, in 1864, establishing rules for the treatment of prisoners of war, the sick, and the wounded.

Human ethics: A form of ethics that assumes, without argument, that only human beings count morally or have moral status. See: **Moral status**.

Hypothetical imperatives: Hypothetical imperatives require that we will the means to the ends that we are committed to achieving (Kant).

Individualism and holism: In environmental ethics, individualism tends to favor the good of the individual more than holism does. By contrast, holism tends to favor the good of the whole more than individualism does.

Inherent value: Having inherent value is roughly the same as having moral status. See: **Moral status**.

Libertarianism: A political view that takes liberty to be the ultimate ideal.

Moral status: Those with moral status cannot be used simply as a means to serve the interests of others.

Negative welfare right: A right not to be interfered with in acquiring the goods and services that are required for basic welfare. See: **Positive welfare right**.

No-conflict thesis: The thesis that there are no real conflicts of interest among rational persons.

Nonquestion-beggingness, Principle of: This principle requires that when we argue, we should not assume in our premises what we are trying to establish in our conclusion.

Original position: In John Rawls's theory of justice, it is the hypothetical position we should choose from when trying to determine what fundamental rights and duties people should have. It is principally characterized by a veil of ignorance. See: **Veil of ignorance**.

Positive welfare right: A right to receive the goods and services required for basic welfare. See: **Negative welfare right**.

Prima facie case: A case for which there is sufficient initial evidence to constitute a proof unless that evidence can be rebutted by the introduction of additional evidence.

Procedural and substantive reasons: Procedural reasons are reasons that support some outcome or decision because of the procedures that were used to arrive at it. Substantive reasons are reasons that (strongly) support some outcome or decision independently of the procedures that we used to arrive at it.

Public reason: A framework of reasons that others can reasonably be expected to endorse.

Speciesism: An unfair favoring of the members of one species over the members of other species.

Suttee: A traditional Hindu practice, now against the law, but sometimes practiced nonetheless, in which a widow allows herself to be cremated alive at her husband's funeral.

Traditional and expanded "Ought" implies "Can" principles: The traditional principle maintains that if we ought to do a particular action, it cannot be logically, physically, or psychologically impossible for us to do that action. The expanded principle simply includes the further restriction that if we ought to do a particular action, it also cannot be unreasonable to require us to do that action.

Universalizability: There are different senses of universalizability. For Kant, universalizability requires that one be able to consistently will one's maxims to be universal laws. For others, egoists in particular, universalizability simply requires that we recognize that if our own actions are justified then the same actions performed by others are justified as well.

Veil of ignorance: In Rawls's theory of justice, the veil of ignorance requires that we discount certain knowledge about ourselves, such as our native abilities, our sex, and social status, when utilizing Rawls's original position and trying to determine what fundamental rights and duties people should have.

Welfare liberalism: A political view that attempts to combine a commitment to liberty with a commitment to insuring the welfare of the poor.

Western and non-Western cultures: For the purposes of this book, Western culture is the dominant modern culture of Europe, North America, Australia, and New Zealand. Non-Western culture is exemplified by the dominant cultures found everywhere else.

INDEX

Page numbers followed by "n" indicate notes.

A

Abraham (Biblical figure), 6–7
Action-tolerance, 24
Adams, Robert, 81, 83
Adultery, 7
Agnostics, 6, 20n1
Agostini v. Felton, 16, 21n18
Alexander the Great, 78
Alien perspective, 104–106. *See also* Environmentalism
al-Qaeda, 55
al-Shehhi, Marwan, 54
Altruistic perspective. *See* Egoistic perspective
Altruistic reaons, 45–47
American Holocaust, 23, 36n3
American Indians, 2–3, 23, 124–126
as Buffalo Commons, 132
culture, 124–126
extermination/removal of, 23, 36n3, 128–132
Jews Holocaust *vs.,* 131
on Pine Ridge Reservation, 2–3, 130
restoring lands of, 132
treaties with, 131–132
American Office of Strategic Services (OSS), 134
Analects, 126, 127
Androgyny, 118
Animal experimentation, 95
Animal exploitation, 95
Animal liberation, 95–96
"Animal Liberation," (Singer), 95
Annas, Julia, 81
Aquinas, Thomas, 7, 20n4
Aramony, William, 37
Aristotelian ethics, 4
actions and, 82–83
Kantian ethics *vs.,* 81–82
of Rand, Ann. *See* Rand, Ayn
rules and, 82
virtuous life and happiness, 78–81
Aristotle, 1, 78. *See also* Aristotelian ethics
Atheists, 6, 20n1
Atlas Shrugged (Rand), 84

Atta, Muhamed, 54
Attlee, Clement, 134

B

Ba'ath party, 135
Baier, Kurt, 42
Basic needs, 73, 74, 75, 77n15
Benedict, Ruth, 24, 36n5
Bennett, William, 122
Bentham, Jeremy, 52–53
Bin Laden, Osama, 55, 56
Biocentrism, 96–98
Buckley, William, 122
Buffalo Commons, 132. *See also* American Indians
Bush, George W., 135
Bybee, Jay, 54
Byrnes, James, 134

C

Callatiae, 25
Card, Claudia, 111
Care perspective, 109–111
Categorical Imperative test (Kant), 65–66
egoism and, 67
formulations of, 68–69
universalizability, 68
Chalabi, Ahmed, 135
Cheney, Dick, 51, 55, 58
Cherokees, 129
Children, American Indians, 130
China, and Vietnam, 133–135
Chinese culture, 126–128
Christian moral teachings, 17
Churchill, Ward, 128, 131–132
Commands of God. *See* Divine command theory
Conflict of interest, in *The Fountainhead* (Rand), 87–88
Conflict of liberties, 73
Conflicts, among God's command, 9
Confucianism, 52
Confucius, 126–128
Copernicus, 1
Courage, 79
Creation, God's commands justified by, 9–10. *See also* Divine command theory

Critique of Practical Reason (Kant), 65
Culture. *See also* Multiculturalism
American Indians, 124–126. *See also* American Indians
Chinese, 126–128
Western and non-Western, 122–124

D

Darius the Great, King of Persia, 22
Discrimination, and feminism, 112–115
Divine command theory, 20n1
identifying commands, 10–11
medieval developments of, 7
morality and, 7–8
moral relativism *vs.,* 33
problems for, 8–11
understanding commands, 8–9
Draize eye test, 95

E

Egoism, 37–50
Ethical. *See* Ethical Egoism
Kantian ethics and, 66–67
Morality as Compromise and, 47–48
Psychological, 37–39
Egoistic perspective, 46, 50n4
Employment Division v. Smith, 16, 21n17
Environmentalism, 95–108
alien perspective, 104–106
biocentrism, 96–98
individualism and holism, 101–104
Kantian, by Regan, 96
overview, 95
Principle of Disproportionality, 100
Principle of Human Defense, 100–101
Principle of Human Preservation, 98–100
Principle of Rectification, 101
utilitarian, by Singer, 95–96

Eskimos (Inuit), 22–23
Ethical Egoism, 39–41
  Individual, 39–40
  publicity requirement and, 41
  racism and, 41–42
  Universal. *See* Universal
    Ethical Egoism
Ethics
  challenges to, 3, 5
  knowledge acquisition, 2–3
  overview, 1
  traditional perspectives, 4
Euthyphro (Plato), 6–7
Evans, Stephen, 11, 20n6

F
Factory farming, 95
Female circumcision, 27, 34,
    36n15–36n22
  justifications for, 31–32
  and moral relativism, 27,
    31–33
Feminism, 109–121
  care and justice perspectives
    and, 109–111
  discrimination and, 112–115
  Gilligan's challenge, 109–111
  morally good person, 115–118
  theories of justice, 111–115
Filial piety, 127
*Foundations of a Metaphysics
    of Morals* (Kant), 65
The Fountainhead (Rand),
    84, 85
  conflict of interest in, 87–88
Francon, Dominique, 85
Freuchen, Peter, 22, 35n2

G
Gender roles, and traits,
    116–117
Geneva Conventions, 51
Gilligan, Carol, 109–111
God's commands. *See* Divine
    command theory
Greeks, 25
*Groundwork of a Metaphysics
    of Morals* (Kant), 81
Guardianship rights, 10
Guerrilla warfare, 133

H
Happiness, and virtuous life,
    78–81
Hayek, F. A., 70–71
Held, Virginia, 110–111
Herodotus, 22, 35n1
Himmler, Heinrich, 131
Ho Chi Minh, 133–134, 135
Holism, and individualism,
    101–104

Holmes, Oliver Wendel, 130
Holocaust, 23, 131
Hospers, John, 71
Howells, William Dean, 130
Human ethics, 97, 107n5
  principle of self-defense
    in, 101
  principle of self-preservation
    in, 98
Human production, 10
Hume, David, 52, 53
Hursthouse, Rosalind, 83
Hussein, Saddam, 135
Hutchinson, Francis, 52
Hypothetical imperatives, 67

I
Ideal of androgyny, 118
In a Different Voice (Gilligan),
    109–111
Indian Territory of Oklahoma,
    129
"Indian Wars," 130
Individual Ethical Egoism,
    39–40. *See also* Ethical
    Egoism
Individualism and holism,
    101–104
Inherent value, 96
Intellectual virtues, 79
Inuit. *See* Eskimos (Inuit)
Iraq, U.S. invasion of, 135,
    137n35
Iroquois, 129

J
Jackson, Andrew, 129
Jen, 127. *See also Li*
Jews, 131
John, Chivington, 130
Judgmental tolerance, 24
Justice perspective, 109–111

K
Kalin, Jesse, 43
Kant, Immanuel, 1, 65.
    See also Kantian ethics
Kantian environmentalism
    (Regan), 96
Kantian ethics, 4, 65–77
  Categorical Imperative
    test. *See* Categorical
    Imperative test (Kant)
  egoism, 66–67
  hypothetical imperatives, 67
  libertarianism, 70–71
  moral requirements, 67
  supporting examples, 71–76
  universalizability, 68
  welfare liberalism, 69–70
Kanwan, Roop, 27, 30, 34

Keating, Peter, 85
Khan, Genghis, 133
Kingston, Maxine Hong,
    127–128
Korsgaard, Christine, 41
Kung Fu-Tzu. *See* Confucius

L
LD50 toxicity test, 95
Leibniz, 126
Li, 127. *See also Jen*
Libertarianism, 70–76. *See also*
    Kantian ethics
  conflict, 73
  "Ought" implies "Can"
    principle, 73–74
  supporting examples, 71–76
Lifeboat cases, 47
Lincoln, Abraham, 38–39
Luxury needs, 73, 74, 75, 100
Lyceum, 78

M
MacIntyre, Alasdair, 80
Madoff, Bernard, 39
Mao Tse-tung, 133
Melodia, Filippo, 26, 28–30,
    34. *See also* Viola, Franca
Metaphysics of Morals (Kant),
    65
Mill, John Stuart, 1, 52, 53
Morality
  being dependent on God,
    7–8
  divine command theory and.
    See Divine command
    theory
  Euthyphro question and, 6–7
Morality as Compromise,
    47–48
Moral judgments, 109
Morally good person, 115–118
  in Aristotelian ethics, 116
  in Kantian ethics, 115–116
  in utilitarian ethics, 116
Moral reasons. *See* Altruistic
    reasons
Moral relativism, 22–36, 122
  criticism of, 33–34
  divine command theory
    vs., 33
  female circumcision, case
    and analysis, 27,
    31–33, 34
  negative consequences, 23
  rape and marriage, case and
    analysis, 16, 28–30, 34
  tolerance and, 23–25
  widow and suttee, case and
    analysis, 27, 30, 34
Moral status, 96–98

Moral virtues, 79
Mo Tzu, 52
Multiculturalism, 122–135.
    See also Culture

N

Nazi Germany, 23, 24
Negative welfare right, 75–76.
    See also Positive welfare
    right
Newton, Isaac, 1
New York Review of Books, 95
Nicomachean Ethics
    (Aristotle), 78
No-conflict thesis, 85–87.
    See also Rand, Ayn
    rejecting, 89–90
No-duty thesis, 88–89. *See also*
    Rand, Ayn
Nonbasic needs. *See* Luxury
    needs
Non-question-begging
    arguments, 44, 47, 96–97
Non-Western cultures,
    122–124. *See also*
    Multiculturalism; Western
    cultures
    American Indians. *See*
    American Indians
    Vietnam, 133–135
Nozick, Robert, 71
Nussbaum, Martha, 80

O

OSS. *See* American Office of
    Strategic Services (OSS)
"Ought" implies "Can"
    principle, 60–62, 64n10,
    93, 99, 116
    libertarianism and, 73–74

P

Philip of Macedon, 78
Philosophical Radicals, 52
Pine Ridge Reservation, 2–3,
    130
Ponzi scheme, 39, 48n4
Popper, Deborah, 132
Popper, Frank, 132
Positive welfare right, 75–76.
    See also Negative welfare
    right
Prima facie relevance, 45,
    50n24
Principle of
    Disproportionality, 100
Principle of Human Defense,
    100–101
Principle of Human
    Preservation, 98–100
Principle of Rectification, 101

*The Principles of Morals and
    Legislation* (Bentham), 52
Private arena, 12, 20n7
Procedural reasons, 15–16,
    17, 18
Procreation, 10
Property rights, 10
Psychological Egoism, 37–39
Ptolemy, 1
Public arena, 11–13, 20n8
Publicity, and Ethical Egoism,
    41
Public reason, 11–18
    accessibility of, 18
    religious moral teachings
    and, 17
    unfairness, 13–16

R

Rachels, James, 24, 36n5,
    41–42
Racism, Ethical Egoism and,
    41–42
Rand, Ayn, 84–90
    on conflict of interest, 87–88
    no-conflict thesis of, 85–87,
    89–90
    no-duty thesis of, 88–89
Rape and marriage, and moral
    relativism, 26, 28–30
Rawls, John, 20n8, 49n8
    on Kant's Categorical
    Imperative, 69
    on public reason, 11–18
    theory of justice. *See A
    Theory of Justice* (Rawls)
    on welfare liberal
    perspective, 69, 70
Regan, Tom, 96
Religion, 11–18
    moral teachings, 17
    public reason and. *See*
    Public reason
Religious moral teachings, 17,
    21n20. *See also* Christian
    moral teachings
The Republic (Plato), 37, 48n1
Revelations. *See* Special
    revelations
Romer v. Evans, 16, 21n19
Roosevelt, Franklin Delano, 133
Roosevelt, Theodore, 130
Royal Chitwan National Park
    in Nepal, 99
Rules of the road, moral
    relativism and, 25, 34

S

Self-interest, 38
    and altruistic reasons, 44–46
Selfishness, virtue theory of, 84

Shackleton, Ernest, 26
Sheridan, Philip, 130
Singer, Peter, 95–96
Special revelations, 10–11.
    See also Divine command
    theory
"Speciesism," 95
Speusippus, 78
Springfield Monitor, 38
Stalin, Joseph, 134
The Subjection of Women
    (Mill), 53
Substantive reasons, 15–16,
    17, 18
Suicide rate, teenage, 2, 130
Sullivan, General John, 129
Suttee (practice), moral
    relativism and, 27, 30, 34,
    36n13

T

Taking-Stock Interlude, 4,
    93–94
Teenage suicide rate, 2, 130
Terrorism, 54–55
Theories of justice, 111–115
A Theory of Justice (Rawls),
    69, 111, 120n14
Third Reich, 24
Tolerance, and moral
    relativism, 23–25
    action-tolerance, 24
    judgment tolerance, 24
Torture, 51, 52, 53–54, 55, 58,
    64n6
Tosawi, Chief of the
    Comanches, 130
"Town Destroyer," 129
Trail of Tears, 129
Traits, gender roles and,
    116–117
Treaty of Fort Wise, 131
Trieu Da, 133

U

UN Convention Against
    Torture, 51
United Way of America, 37,
    48n2
Universal Ethical Egoism,
    40–41. *See also* Ethical
    Egoism
    challenge of, 43–47
    consistency and, 42–43
    lifeboat cases, 47
    publicity requirement and, 41
    rationality and, 44–46
U.S. Constitution, 17
U.S. Family and Medical Leave
    Act of 1993, 114
U.S. judiciary, 9

Utilitarian ethics, 51–64
  concept of, 52–53
  hypothetical example, 56
  implications of, 53–54
  objection to, 57–59
  "Ought" implies "Can"
    principle, 60–62
  overview, 51–52
  terrorism and, 54–55
  torture in. *See* Torture

V

Valadez, Jorge, 125, 136n8
Veil of ignorance, 69, 70, 111,
  115

Viet Minh, 133–135
Vietnam
  history of, 133
  U.S. involvement in, 133–135
Viola, Franca, 26, 28–30, 34.
    See also Melodia, Filippo
Virtue, 79
The Virtue of Selfishness
    (Rand), 84
Virtuous life, and happiness,
  78–81

W

Washington, George, 129
Waterhouse, Edward, 128

Welfare liberalism, 69–70.
    See also Kantian ethics
Western cultures, 122–124.
    See also Multiculturalism
Widows and suttee. *See*
    Suttee (practice), moral
    relativism and
Will, George, 122
William of Ockham, 7, 20n3
Wolff, Christian, 126
Wolterstorff, Nicholas,
  12–13
Woman Warrior (Kingston),
  127–128
Wu-ti, 133